The Future of Banking

A VoxEU.org Book

Centre for Economic Policy Research (CEPR)

Centre for Economic Policy Research
3rd Floor
77 Bastwick Street
London, EC1V 3PZ
UK

Tel: +44 (0)20 7183 8801
Fax: +4 (0)20 7183 8820
Email: cepr@cepr.org
Web: www.cepr.org

ISBN (print edition): 978-1-907142-47-5

The Future of Banking

A VoxEU.org Book

Edited by Thorsten Beck

Centre for Economic Policy Research (CEPR)

The Centre for Economic Policy Research is a network of over 700 Research Fellows and Affiliates, based primarily in European Universities. The Centre coordinates the research activities of its Fellows and Affiliates and communicates the results to the public and private sectors. CEPR is an entrepreneur, developing research initiatives with the producers, consumers and sponsors of research. Established in 1983, CEPR is a European economics research organization with uniquely wide-ranging scope and activities.

The Centre is pluralist and non-partisan, bringing economic research to bear on the analysis of medium- and long-run policy questions. CEPR research may include views on policy, but the Executive Committee of the Centre does not give prior review to its publications, and the Centre takes no institutional policy positions. The opinions expressed in this report are those of the authors and not those of the Centre for Economic Policy Research.

CEPR is a registered charity (No. 287287) and a company limited by guarantee and registered in England (No. 1727026).

Contents

Foreword

During the three years that have elapsed since the collapse of Lehman Brothers in 2008 – an event which heralded the most serious global financial crisis since the 1930s – CEPR's policy portal Vox, under the editorial guidance of Richard Baldwin, has produced 15 books on crisis-related issues written by world-leading economists and specialists. The books have been designed to shed light on the problems related to the crisis and to provide expert advice and guidance for policy makers on potential solutions.

The Vox books are produced rapidly and are timed to 'catch the wave' as the issue under discussion reaches its high point of debate amongst world leaders and decision makers. The topic of this book is no exception to that pattern. European leaders are gathering this weekend in Brussels to search for a solution to the Eurozone debt crisis – proposals for the recapitalisation of Europe's banks are high on the agenda.

Whilst many people were of the opinion that the banking crisis was more or less resolved two years ago and that the more pressing issue to tackle was the emerging sovereign debt crisis and the risk of contagion, the full extent to which sovereign risk and banking risk are in reality so dangerously intertwined has become increasingly clear – no big European bank is now safe from the potential impact of holding bad government debt.

This Vox book presents a collection of essays by leading European and US economists that offer solutions to the crisis and proposals for medium- to long-term reforms to the regulatory framework in which financial institutions operate. Amongst other proposals, the authors present the case for a forceful resolution of the Eurozone crisis through the introduction of 'European Safe Bonds' (ESBies). They discuss capital and liquidity requirements and maintain that risk weights that are dynamic, counter-cyclical and take into account the co-dependence of financial institutions are crucial, and that liquidity requirements should be adjusted to make them less rigid and pro-cyclical. The relationship of bank tax and risk-taking behaviour is also analysed.

An important question in the banking debate is whether regulation is stimulating or hindering retail banking, and what the potential implications are of multiple, but uncoordinated, reform frameworks, such as the Basel III requirements, the Capital Requirements Directive IV in Europe, the Dodd-Frank Act in the US, and the Independent Commission on Banking Report in the UK, etc? There is a call for more joined-up thinking and action in banking regulatory reform and the authors in this book stress the need for a stronger, European-wide regulatory framework as well as for a European-level resolution authority for systemically important financial institutions (SIFIs).

Whilst it is important that policy makers ensure that regulation serves to stabilise the banking sector and make it more resilient, the authors remind us that it is equally, if not more, important to ensure that we do not forget the essential role of banks in terms of their vital contribution to the 'real economy' and the pivotal role they play as lenders to small- and medium-size enterprises in support of economic growth at local and regional levels.

We are grateful to Thorsten Beck for his enthusiasm and energy in organising and co-ordinating the inputs to this book; we are also grateful to the authors of the papers for their rapid responses to the invitation to contribute. As ever, we also gratefully acknowledge the contribution of Team Vox (Jonathan Dingel, Samantha Reid and Anil Shamdasani) who produced the book with characteristic speed and professionalism.

What began as a banking crisis in 2008, symbolised by the collapse of Lehman Brothers, soon became a sovereign debt crisis in Europe, which in turn has precipitated a further banking crisis with potentially massive global implications; if European banks fail then there will also be serious repercussions for Asian and US lenders too. Effectively, Europe's problem is now the world's problem. It is our sincere hope that this Vox book helps towards clarifying the way forward.

Viv Davies

Chief Operating Officer, CEPR

24 October 2011

The future of banking – solving the current crisis while addressing long-term challenges

Thorsten Beck
Tilburg University and CEPR

For better or worse, banking is back in the headlines. From the desperate efforts of crisis-struck Eurozone governments to the Occupy Wall Street movement currently spreading across the globe, the future of banking is hotly debated. This VoxEU.org eBook presents a collection of essays by leading European and American economists that discuss both immediate solutions to the on-going financial crisis and medium- to long-term regulatory reforms.

Three years after the Lehman Brothers failure sent shockwaves through financial markets, banks are yet again in the centre of the storm. While in 2008 financial institutions "caused" the crisis and triggered widespread bailouts followed by fiscal stimulus programmes to limit the fall-out of the banking crisis for the rest of the economy, banks now seem to be more on the receiving end. The sovereign debt crisis in several southern European countries and potential large losses from a write-down of Greek debt make the solvency position of many European banks doubtful, which in turn explains the limited funding possibilities for many banks. As pointed by out many economists, including Charles Wyplosz in this collection of essays, policy mistakes have made a bad situation even worse.

The outrage over "yet another bank bailout" is justified. The fact that banks are yet again in trouble shows that the previous crisis of 2008 has not been used sufficiently to fix the underlying problems. If politicians join the outcry, however, it will be hypocritical because it was they, after all, who did not use the last crisis sufficiently for the necessary reforms. After a short period in crisis mode, there was too much momentum to go back to the old regime, with only minor changes here and there. This is not too say that I am advocating "radical" solutions such as nationalisation. This is not exactly radical, as it has been tried extensively across the world and has failed. But wouldn't it actually be radical to force financial institutions to internalise the external costs that risk-taking decisions and their failure impose on the rest of the economy? So rather than moving from "privatising profits and nationalising losses" to nationalising both, I would advocate privatising both (which might also reduce both profits and losses!) – an old idea that has not really been popular among policy makers these past years in the industrialised world. An idea that some observers might call naïve, but maybe an idea whose time has finally come.

A call for action

Before discussing in more depth the main messages of this eBook, let me point to three headline messages:

1. We need a forceful and swift resolution of the Eurozone crisis, without further delay! For this to happen, the sovereign debt and banking crises that are intertwined have to be addressed with separate policy tools. This concept finally seems to have dawned on policymakers. Now it is time to follow up on this insight and to be resolute.
2. It's all about incentives! We have to think beyond mechanical solutions that create cushions and buffers (exact percentage of capital requirements or net funding ratios) to incentives for financial institutions. How can regulations (capital, liquidity, tax, activity restrictions) be shaped in a way that forces financial institutions to internalise all repercussions of their risk, especially the external costs of their potential failure?
3. It is the endgame, stupid. The interaction between banks and regulators/politicians is a multi-round game. As any game theorist will tell you, it is best to solve this from the end. A bailout upon failure will provide incentives for aggressive risk-taking throughout the life of a bank. Only a credible resolution regime that forces risk

decision-takers to bear the losses of these decisions is an incentive compatible with aligning the interests of banks and the broader economy.

The Eurozone crisis – lots of ideas, little action

One of the important characteristics of the current crisis is that there are actually two crises ongoing in Europe – a sovereign debt and a bank crisis – though the two are deeply entangled. Current plans to use the EFSF to recapitalise banks, however, might not be enough, as there are insufficient resources under the plans. Voluntary haircuts will not be sufficient either; they rather constitute a bank bailout through the back door. Many policy options have been suggested over the past year to address the European financial crisis but, as time has passed, some of these are no longer feasible given the worsening situation. It is now critical that decisions are taken rapidly, the incurred losses are recognised and distributed clearly, and banks are either recapitalised where possible or resolved where necessary.

Comparisons have been made to the Argentine crisis of 2001 (Levy Yeyati, Martinez Peria, and Schmukler 2011), and lessons on the effect of sovereign default on the banking system can certainly be learned. The critical differences are obviously the much greater depth of the financial markets in Greece and across the Eurozone, and the much greater integration of Greece, which would turn a disorderly Greek default into a major global financial shock. Solving a triple crisis such as Greece's – sovereign debt, banking, and competitiveness – is more complicated in the case of a member of a currency union and, even though Greece constitutes only 2% of Eurozone GDP, the repercussions of the Greek crisis for the rest of the Eurozone and the global economy are enormous (similar to the repercussions of problems in the relatively small subprime mortgage segment in the US for global finance in 2007-8).

One often-discussed policy option to address the sovereign debt crisis is creating euro bonds, i.e. joint liability of Eurozone governments for jointly issued bonds. In addition to their limited desirability, given the moral hazard risk they are raising, their political feasibility in the current environment is doubtful. Several economists have therefore suggested alternatives, which would imply repackaging existing debt securities into a debt mutual fund structure (Beck, Uhlig and Wagner 2011), or issuing ESBies funded by currently outstanding government debt up to 60% of GDP, a plan detailed by Markus Brunnermeier and co-authors in this book. By creating a large pool of safe assets – about half the size of US Treasuries – this proposal would help with both liquidity and solvency problems of the European banking system and, most critically, help to distinguish between the two. Obviously, this is only one step in many, but it could help to separate the sovereign debt crisis from the banking crisis and would allow the ECB to disentangle more clearly liquidity support for the banks from propping up insolvent governments in the European periphery.

Regulatory reform – good start, but only half-way there

After the onset of the global financial crisis, there was a lot of talk about not wasting the crisis, but rather using it to push through the necessary regulatory reforms. And there have been reforms, most prominently the Dodd-Frank Act in the US. Other countries are still discussing different options, such as the recommendations of the Vickers report in the UK. Basel III, with new capital and liquidity requirements, is set to replace Basel II, though with long transition periods. Economists have been following this reform process and many have concluded that, while important steps have been taken, many reforms are only going half-way or do not take into account sufficiently the interaction of different regulatory levers.

The crisis has shed significant doubts on the inflation paradigm – the dominant paradigm for monetary policy prior to the crisis – as it does not take into account financial stability challenges. Research summarised by Steven Ongena and José-Luis Peydró clearly shows the important effect that monetary policy, working through short-term interest rates, has on banks' risk-taking and, ultimately, bank fragility. Additional policy levers, such as counter-cyclical capital requirements, are therefore needed.

The 2008 crisis has often been called the grave of market discipline, as one large financial institution after another was bailed out and the repercussions of the one major exception – Lehman Brothers' bankruptcy – ensured that policymakers won't use that instrument any time soon. But can we really rely on market discipline for systemic discipline? As Arnoud Boot points out, from a macro-prudential view (i.e. a system-wide view) market discipline is not effective. While it can work for idiosyncratic risk choices of an individual financial institution, herding effects driven by momentum in financial markets make market discipline ineffective for the overall system.

Ring-fencing – the separation of banks' commercial and trading activities, known as the Volcker Rule but also recommended by the Vickers Commission – continues to be heavily discussed. While Boot thinks that "heavy-handed intervention in the structure of the banking industry … is an inevitable part of the restructuring of the industry", Viral Acharya insists that it is not a panacea. Banks might still undertake risky activities within the ring. Capital requirements might be more important, but more important still than the actual level of such requirements is the question of whether the current risk weights are correct. For example, risk weights for sovereign debt have certainly been too low, as we can see in the current crisis in Europe. Critically, we need to fundamentally rethink the usefulness of static risk weights, which do not change when the market's risk assessment of an asset class permanently changes. In addition, capital requirements have to take into account the co-dependence of financial institutions, as pointed out by Acharya and Matthew Richardson. This would lead to systemic risk surcharges, though they might not necessarily be perfectly correlated with the size of financial institutions. And whatever is being decided for the banking sector should trigger comparable regulation for the shadow banking sector to avoid simply shifting risk outside the regulatory perimeter.

Tweaking different levers of the regulatory framework independent of each other can, however, create more risk instead of mitigating it. Capital requirements and activity restrictions that do not take into account the governance and ownership structure of banks can easily have counterproductive effects, as Luc Laeven argues. Stricter capital regulations can actually result in greater risk-taking when the bank has a sufficiently powerful and diversified owner, but have the opposite effect in widely held banks. A one-size-fits-all approach is therefore not appropriate.

Another area of reform has been liquidity requirements, recognised as the biggest gap in Basel II. Enrico Perotti, however, points out that the suggested reforms – liquidity coverage ratios (buffers of liquid assets as a fraction of less stable funding) and net funding ratios (quantitative limits to short-term funding) – are (a) too rigid, (b) procyclical, and (c) distortionary against efficient lenders. He rather recommends using those ratios as long-term targets while imposing “prudential risk surcharges” on deviations from the targets.

Taxation of banks – why settle for fourth-best?

For many years, taxation of financial institutions was a topic for specialists, as much among tax or public finance economists as among financial economists. The current crisis and the need for large recapitalisation amounts for banks have changed this dramatically, and taxation for banks now forms part of a broader debate on regulatory reform. Proposals to introduce a financial transaction tax, in one form or another, have emerged in the political arena over the past three years with a regularity that matches seasonal changes in Europe. As Harry Huizinga and I point out, such a tax would not significantly affect banks’ risk-taking behaviour. Rather, it might actually increase market volatility and its revenue potential might be overestimated. Banks are under-taxed, but there are better ways to address this gap, such as eliminating the VAT exemption on financial services or a common EU framework for bank levies.

Looking beyond national borders

Cross-border banking in Europe can only survive with a move of regulation and resolution of cross-border banks to the European level, as emphasised by Dirk Schoenmaker. If the common market in banking is to be saved, the geographic perimeter of banks has to be matched with a similar geographic perimeter in regulation, which ultimately requires new European-level institutions. Many of the reforms being discussed or already implemented, including macro-prudential tools and bank resolution, have to be at least coordinated if not implemented at the European level (Allen et al. 2011). Critically, the resolution of financial institutions has an important cross-border element to it. In 2008, authorities had limited choices when it came to intervening and resolving failing banks and, in the case of cross-border banks, resolution had to be nationalised. Progress has been made in the reform of bank resolution, both in the context of the Dodd-Frank Act and in the preparation of living wills. More remains to be done, especially on the cross-border level.

While most of the discussion is currently on banking system reform in the US and Europe, we should not ignore trends in the emerging world. As Neeltje van Horen points out in her contribution, among the global top 25 banks (as measured by market capitalisation), there are 8 emerging-market banks, including 4 Chinese, 3 Brazilian, and 1 Russian. Due to their sheer size, emerging-market banks will almost undoubtedly soon become important players in the world's financial system. And given that US and European banks are still to adjust to the new rules of the game, large banks from the emerging countries are likely to step into the void left by advanced-country banks. There will be a continuing shift towards emerging markets also in banking!

Why do we care?

Above all, however, it is important to remind ourselves of why we care about the banking sector in the first place. Given the roles of credit default swaps, collateralised debt obligations, and other new financial instruments in the recent financial crisis, financial innovation has garnered a bad reputation. But in his contribution, Ross Levine reminds us of the powerful role of financial innovation through history in enabling economic growth and the introduction of new products and providers in the real economy. Financial innovation fosters financial deepening and broadening. Rather than stifling it, we have to harness it for the benefit of the real economy.

References

Allen, Franklin, Thorsten Beck, Elena Carletti, Philip Lane, Dirk Schoenmaker and Wolf Wagner (2011), *Cross-border banking in Europe: implications for financial stability and macroeconomic policies*. CEPR.

Beck, Thorsten, Harald Uhlig and Wolf Wagner (2011), "Insulating the financial sector from the European debt crisis: Eurobonds without public guarantee", VoxEU.org.

Levy Yeyati, Eduardo, Maria Soledad Martinez Peria and Sergio Schmukler (2011), "Triplet Crises and the Ghost of the New Drachma", VoxEU.org.

About the author

Thorsten Beck is Professor of Economics and Chairman of the European Banking CentER at Tilburg University, and a CEPR Research Fellow. His research and policy work has focused on international banking and corporate finance.

Resolving the current European mess

Charles Wyplosz
Graduate Institute, Geneva and CEPR

A series of policy mistakes have put Europe on the wrong path. This chapter says that the current plan to enlarge the EFSF and recapitalise banks through markets will fail. The twin crises linking sovereign debts and banking turmoil need to be addressed simultaneously for Europe to avoid economic disaster.

Invariably, policy mistakes make a bad situation worse. The May 2010 rescue package was officially designed to prevent contagion within the Eurozone, but the crisis has been spreading ever since, as evidenced by the interest spreads over German ten-year bond rates (Figure 1). Unofficially, a number of governments were concerned about exposure of their banks to Greek and other potential crisis-countries' bonds. Banks are now in crisis, a striking blow to the July stress tests that were officially intended to reassure the world and unofficially designed to deliver reassuring results. This is not just denial; it is an attempted cover-up.

The debate is now whether it is more urgent to solve the sovereign debt crisis or the banking crisis. The obvious answer is that these two crises are deeply entangled and that both crises must be solved simultaneously. Debt defaults will impose punishing costs on banks, while bank failures will require costly bailouts that will push more countries onto the hit list. Spain, Italy, Belgium, and France are on the brink. Quite possibly, Germany might join the fray if some of its large banks fail. This should dispel any hope that Germany will bankroll governments and banks. German taxpayers are revolting against more bailouts, but they may not realise that they cannot even afford to be the white knight of Europe. From this, a number of conclusions follow.

Figure 1. Ten-year bond spreads over German bonds (basis points)

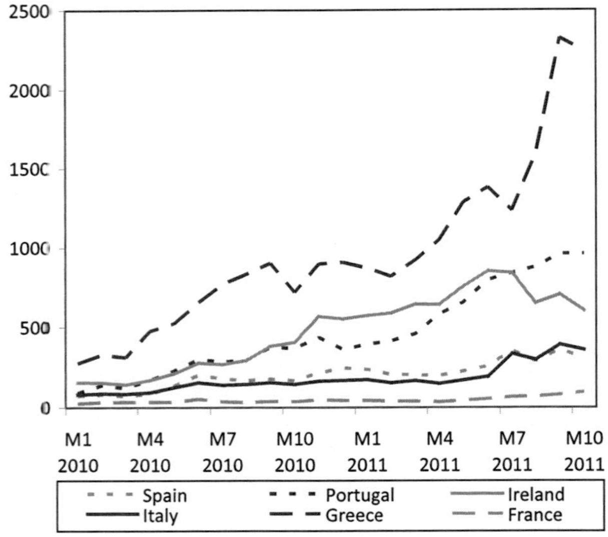

Conclusion 1 is that current policy preoccupation with widening the role of the EFSF and enlarging its resources is bound to disappoint and trigger yet another round of market panic. Unofficial estimates of how much more capital the banks included in the European stress test need to restore market confidence (ie aligning their Tier 1 capital to banks currently considered safe) range from $400 to $1000 billion. Even if the EFSF can lend a total to $440 billion, with some €100 billion already earmarked for Ireland and Portugal, this is not enough to deal just with the banking crisis.

The current plan is for banks to seek fresh capital from the markets, with EFSF resources as a backstop. Conclusion 2 is that this plan will not work. Markets are worrying about the impact of contagious government defaults on banks. They will not buy into banks that are about to suffer undefined losses. Somehow, a price tag, even highly approximate, must be tacked on sovereign defaults for investors to start thinking about acquiring bank shares. They need to know which governments will default and in what proportion. Since this will not be announced *ex ante,* market-based bank recapitalisation is merely wishful thinking. Much the same applies to the much-talked-about support from China, Brazil, and other friends of Europe. They well understand that they stand to throw good money after bad and will not do so unless they can extract serious political concessions. One cannot imagine how much several hundred billions of euros are politically worth.

Assuming that, somehow, bank recapitalisation and debt defaults can be handled simultaneously (more on that later), how to make defaults reasonably orderly? Last July, the European Council set the parameters of an orderly Greek default. Hau (2011) shows that this agreement, dubbed voluntary Private Sector Involvement (PSI), has been masterminded by the banks and only aims at bailing out banks, not at significantly reducing the Greek public debt. Conclusion 3 is that there is no such thing as a voluntary PSI. Banks are not philanthropic institutions; they always fight any potential loss to the last cent. If not, they would have bailed out Lehman Brothers without the US Treasury guarantee that they were denied.

This brings us to Conclusion 4 – in order to avoid a massive financial and economic convulsion, some guarantee must be offered regarding the size of sovereign defaults. Crucially, the country-by-country approach officially followed is unworkable. The current exclusive focus on Greece is wholly inadequate. Markets look at Greece as a template. Whatever solution is applied to Greece will have to be applied to other defaulting countries. Adopting an unrealistically short list of potential defaulters will only raise market alarm and result in failure. Such a list is difficult to establish on pure economic grounds (should Belgium and France be added to Italy and Spain?) and politically explosive (governments cannot provoke a default by including a country in a near-death list). The only feasible solution is to guarantee all public debts, thus avoiding both stigma and lack of credibility. Finland, Estonia and Luxembourg would do the Eurozone an historical service by requesting to be part of a debt guarantee scheme.

What kind of guarantee scheme is needed? An example is provided in Wyplosz (2011). In a nutshell, all sovereign debts must be partially guaranteed (eg up to 60% of each country's GDP, or up to 50% of the nominal value). The scheme would backstop debt prices by setting a floor on potential losses. It would lead to less panicky debt pricing by the markets. In turn these market prices would serve as a guide to debt renegotiation between sovereigns and their creditors. By depoliticizing the process, it would make defaults as orderly as possible under the circumstances.

Who can offer such a guarantee, which is effectively a price guarantee? A price guarantee only operates if markets know beyond doubt that the guarantor can and will buy any bond that trades below the announced target (which in this case is a floor). The total value of Eurozone public debts stands at some €8300 billion (more than three times the German – or Chinese – GDP). This is beyond any enlargement of the EFSF. This is beyond current and future IMF lending resources, currently some €400 billion. The unavoidable conclusion is that the ECB is the only institution in the world that can backstop public debts and make reasonably orderly defaults possible. The current ECB position – "we have done what we can, now it is up to governments" – dramatically misses the point. Of course, the ECB may be concerned about taking on such a momentous task; an imaginative solution is for the ECB to provide the commitment through the EFSF, as suggested by Gros and Maier (2011).

Finally, how can the two rescues – of sovereign debts and banks – be carried out simultaneously, as required? If Greece defaults, its banks, pension funds, and insurance companies will fail in large number. It seems that Greece will not be able to bail them out. Assume, just as an example, that Greece defaults on half of its public debt (about 70% of its GDP). Assume that bailing out its banks, pension funds, and insurance companies costs 30% of GDP. The government can do the bailout and still come out with a debt that is lower than now by 40% of GDP. Greece can afford to borrow what it needs to bail out its financial system. The solution then is that the ECB – directly or indirectly via the EFSF – partially guarantees the existing stock of debts and fully newly issued debts simultaneously. Obviously, the guarantee of future debts cannot be given without absolute and verifiable assurance of fiscal discipline in the future. Proposals to that effect are presented in Wyplosz (2011).

References

Gros, Daniel and Thomas Maier (2011) "Refinancing the EFSF via the ECB", *CEPS Commentaries*, 18 August

Hau, Harald (2011) "Europe's €200 billion reverse wealth tax explained", VoxEU.org, 27 July.

Wyplosz, Charles (2011) "A failsafe way to end the Eurozone crisis", VoxEU. org, 26 September.

About the author

Charles Wyplosz is Professor of International Economics at the Graduate Institute, Geneva; where he is Director of the International Centre for Money and Banking Studies. Previously, he has served as Associate Dean for Research and Development at INSEAD and Director of the PhD program in Economics at the Ecole des Hautes Etudes en Science Sociales in Paris. He has also been Director of the International Macroeconomics Program at CEPR. His main research areas include financial crises, European monetary integration, fiscal policy, economic transition and current regional integration in various parts of the world

ESBies: A realistic reform of Europe's financial architecture

Markus K. Brunnermeier, Luis Garicano, Philip R. Lane, Marco Pagano, Ricardo Reis, Tano Santos, David Thesmar, Stijn Van Nieuwerburgh, and Dimitri Vayanos
Euro-nomics.com and CEPR

How can Europe fix its sovereign-debt crisis? Many favour euro bonds, but those seem politically impractical because they would require supranational fiscal policies. This chapter proposes creating safe European assets without requiring additional funding by having a European debt agency repackage members' debts into `euro-safe-bonds'.

The current European crisis has exposed several flaws in the design of the Eurozone financial system. It was internally inconsistent. On the one hand, it imposed a 'no-bail out clause' ruling out any bailout to ensure that interest rate differentials provide a clear signal about the buildup of imbalances. On the other hand, Basel bank regulations treated sovereign debt essentially as risk-free, implicitly assuming that there would always be a bailout. The latter assumption induced European banks to take on excessive exposure to their own sovereign credit risk. This led to a diabolic loop whereby sovereign risk and bank weakness reinforced each other – in countries where sovereign debt was perceived to be riskier, bank stocks plunged, leading to expectations of a public bailout, further increasing the perceived credit risk in government bonds, as illustrated in the following figure.

Moreover, the current design of the Eurozone promoted excessive capital flows across borders, followed by massive self-fulfilling flight to safety when confidence in a given country's debt is lost. At times of turbulence, investors run from some countries, such as Italy, to park their investment in safe havens, such as German bunds. Seeing their bond price collapsing, these countries have to tighten their budgets, but insofar as this leads to contraction of their economies it validates the market's pessimistic expectations. In the run-up phase, capital flows from Germany into the peripheral countries were excessive, depressing German GDP growth for a decade. All in all, the diversity and cross-country allocation of sovereign bonds made the Eurozone's financial system unstable and led to the current crisis.

Figure 1

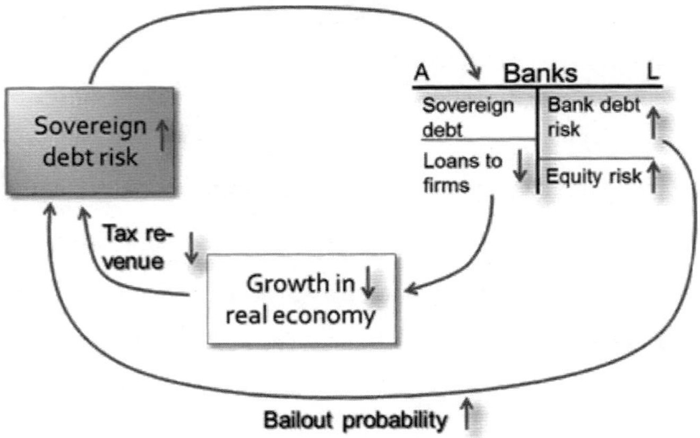

Many analysts, commentators, and policymakers view euro bonds as a solution to these problems. Euro bonds help to reduce the close ties between banks and their own country's sovereign risk, since they make all banks exposed to the same Eurozone-wide risk. Moreover, this risk is lower than in individual bonds since euro bonds enjoy the benefit of diversification. Also, euro bonds break the vicious circle of flight to quality. Finally, euro bonds will be easy to sell – the global demand for safe assets is very high. Many believe that the quasi-monopoly enjoyed by US Treasuries attracted global savings, which in turn made its way to subprime mortgages with well-known consequences. By creating a large-size alternative to US Treasuries, euro bonds will therefore provide stability to the world financial system.

Unfortunately, euro bonds are not politically feasible in the near future. Because they would involve joint and several liability of all member states, euro bonds cannot be set up without a common fiscal policy. National parliaments would be stripped of their most essential function – voting on fiscal policy. Government budgets, before even being discussed by elected representatives, would have to win the approval of a supranational committee where fiscally virtuous countries would have a decisive vote.

Spanish fiscal policy would be partly decided in Brussels. This risks sharply reducing the democratic legitimacy of the European project.

Our proposal, Euro-Safe-Bonds (ESBies), has all the advantages of euro bonds (financial stabilisation of the Eurozone), without its drawbacks (political constraints).[1] ESBies are politically feasible because they involve no joint liability of member states. They imply no change in European treaties. Yet they will generate a very large pool of homogenous, safe assets that can serve as investment vehicles for global investors and reliable collateral for European banks.

Here is our proposal. A European debt agency would buy on the secondary market approximately 5.5 trillion euros of sovereign debt (60% of the Eurozone's GDP). The weight of each country's debt would be equal to its contribution to the Eurozone's GDP. Hence, each marginal euro of sovereign debt beyond 60% of GDP would have to be traded on a single bond market, where prices would reflect true sovereign risk, sending the right signal to the country's government. To finance its 5.5 trillion purchase, the debt agency would issue two securities. The first security, the ESBies, would be senior on interest and principal repayments of bonds held by the agency. The second security would receive the rest – it is therefore riskier and would take the hit if one or more sovereigns default. European banking regulation and ECB policy would be adjusted so that banks face incentives to invest in safe ESBies instead of risky sovereign debt.

According to our calibrations, this mechanism would allow the European debt agency to issue about 3.8 trillion of extremely safe ESBies. Given historical data and conservative assumptions about default correlations, ESBies would default once every 600 years. They would therefore be rated AAA and command a yield similar to (or even below) German bunds. The junior tranche, about 1.7 trillion euros, would yield about 6% in normal times and would be considered investment grade. Institutional investors as well as mutual funds and hedge funds would therefore be willing to buy it.

1 See Brunnermeier et al (2011) for a detailed description of the proposal.

ESBies have many of the advantages of euro bonds. They create a large pool of safe assets, about half the size of US Treasuries, and will therefore stabilise and diversify global capital flows. If, as we propose, ESBies are accepted as collateral by the ECB (they are very safe), European banks will buy them. This will lower the exposure of banks to their own sovereign and break the vicious circle described above. ESBies will bring stability to the financial system. Yet they are politically feasible – because they are a pure repackaging of existing debt, they do not require additional funding by member states. They do not involve joint liability; if one member-state defaults, the junior tranche will take the hit. Finally, because purchases by the debt agency are capped at 60% of the Eurozone's GDP, countries will face their individual credit spreads on all euros borrowed above this limit. Individual market signals will discipline each government. Because they take moral hazard issues seriously, ESBies will not face opposition from public opinions in fiscally responsible countries. No new treaty will need to be ratified.

ESBies are a realistic and feasible proposal to improve the resilience of the Eurozone's financial architecture. They are part of the solution to the current crisis, but they are not the full solution. Getting out of the crisis also requires a combination of sovereign default and bank recapitalisations. Nor are they the only reform needed to stabilise the Eurozone's financial system in the medium run. Hence, ESBies should be implemented along with new European-wide resolution mechanisms for bank failures and sovereign defaults, which we will describe in future papers. The good news is, they are easy to implement and will not face political opposition.

References

Brunnermeier, Markus K, Luis Garicano, Philip R Lane, Marco Pagano, Ricardo Reis, Tano Santos, Stijn Van Nieuwerburgh, and Dimitri Vayanos (2011), "European Safe Bonds: ESBies," *Euro-nomics.com*

About the authors

Markus K. Brunnermeier is the Edwards S. Sanford Professor of Economics at Princeton University and a CEPR Research Fellow. His research focuses on financial markets and the macroeconomy with special emphasis on bubbles, liquidity, financial stability and its implication for financial regulation and monetary policy. His models incorporate frictions as well as behavioral elements.

Luis Garicano is Professor at the London School of Economics, where he holds a Chair in Economics and Strategy at the Departments of Management and of Economics, and a CEPR Research Fellow. His research focuses on the determinants of economic performance at the firm and economy-wide levels, on the consequences of globalization and information technology for economic growth, inequality and productivity, and on the architecture of institutions and economic systems to minimize incentive and bounded rationality problems.

Philip R. Lane is Professor of International Macroeconomics at Trinity College Dublin and a CEPR Research Fellow. His research interests include financial globalisation, the macroeconomics of exchange rates and capital flows, macroeconomic policy design, European Monetary Union, and the Irish economy.

Marco Pagano is Professor of Economics at University of Naples Federico II, President of the Einaudi Institute for Economics and Finance (EIEF) and a CEPR Research Fellow. Most of his research is in the area of financial economics, especially in the fields of corporate finance, banking and stock market microstructure. He has also done research in macroeconomics, especially on its interactions with financial markets.

Ricardo A. M. R. Reis is a Professor of Economics at Columbia University and a CEPR Research Fellow. His main area of research is macroeconomics, both theoretical and applied, and some of his past work has focused on understanding why people are inattentive, why information spreads slowly, inflation dynamics, building better measures of inflation, unconventional monetary policy, and the evaluation of fiscal stimulus programs.

Tano Santos currently holds the David L. and Elsie M. Dodd Professor of Finance and Economics chair at Columbia Business School of Columbia University and is a CEPR Research Fellow. His research focuses in three areas: asset pricing, financial intermediation and organizational economics.

David Thesmar is a Professor of Finance at HEC, Paris, and a Research Fellow at CEPR. His research interests are: behavioral finance, financial intermediation, corporate finance and governance.

Stijn Van Nieuwerburgh is Associate Professor of Finance and the Yamaichi Faculty Fellow at New York University Leonard N. Stern School of Business, and a CEPR Research Fellow. His research lies in the intersection of macroeconomics, asset pricing, and housing. One strand of his work studies how financial market liberalization in the mortgage market relaxed households' down payment constraints, and how that affected the macro-economy, and the prices of stocks and bonds.

Dimitri Vayanos is Professor of Finance at the London School of Economics, where he also directs the Paul Woolley Centre for the Study of Capital Market Dysfunctionality, and a CEPR Research Fellow. His research, published in leading economics and finance journals, focuses on financial markets with frictions, and on the frictions' implications for market liquidity, market anomalies and limits of arbitrage, financial crises, welfare and policy. Vayanos has also worked on behavioral models of belief formation, and on information transmission within organizations.

Loose monetary policy and excessive credit and liquidity risk-taking by banks

Steven Ongena and **José-Luis Peydró**
CentER, Tilburg University; Universitat Pompeu Fabra

Do low interest rates encourage excessive risk-taking by banks? This chapter summarises two studies analysing the impact of short-term interest rates on the risk composition of the supply of credit. They find that lower rates spur greater risk-taking by lower-capitalised banks and greater liquidity risk exposure.

A question under intense academic and policy debate since the start of the ongoing severe financial crisis is whether a low monetary-policy rate spurs excessive risk-taking by banks. From the start of the crisis in the summer of 2007 market commentators were quick to argue that, during the long period of very low interest rates from 2002 to 2005, banks had softened their lending standards and taken on excessive risk.

Indeed, nominal rates were the lowest in almost four decades and below Taylor rates in many countries while real rates were negative (Taylor 2007, Rajan 2010, Reinhart and Rogoff 2010, among others). Expansionary monetary policy and credit risk-taking followed by restrictive monetary policy possibly led to the financial crisis during the 1990s in Japan (Allen and Gale 2004), while lower real interest rates preceded banking crises in 47 countries (von Hagen and Ho 2007). This time the regulatory arbitrage for bank capital associated with the high degree of bank leverage, the widespread use of complex and opaque financial instruments including loan securitization, and the increased interconnectedness among financial intermediaries may have intensified the resultant risk-taking associated with expansive monetary policy (Calomiris 2009, Mian and Sufi 2009, Acharya and Richardson 2010).

During the crisis, commentators also continuously raised concerns that a zero policy interest rate combined with additional and far-reaching quantitative easing, while alleviating the immediate predicament of many financial market participants, were sowing the seeds for the next credit bubble (Giavazzi and Giovannini 2010).

Recent theoretical work has modelled how changes in short-term interest rates may affect credit and liquidity risk-taking by financial intermediaries. Banks may take more risk in their lending when monetary policy is expansive and, especially when afflicted by agency problems, banks' risk-taking can turn excessive.

Indeed, lower short-term interest rates may reduce the threat of deposit withdrawals, and improve banks' liquidity and net worth, allowing banks to relax their lending standards and to increase their credit and liquidity risk-taking. Acute agency problems in banks, when their capital is low for example, combined with a reliance on short-term funding, may therefore lead short-term interest rates – more than long-term rates – to spur risk-taking. Finally, low short-term interest rates make riskless assets less attractive and may lead to a search-for-yield by those financial institutions that have short time horizons.

Concurrent with these theoretical developments, recent empirical work in progress has begun to study the impact of monetary policy on credit risk-taking by banks. Recent papers that in essence study the impact of short-term interest rates on the risk composition of the supply of credit follow a longstanding and wide literature that has analysed its impact on the aggregate volume of credit in the economy, and on the changes in the composition of credit in response to changes in the quality of the pool of borrowers.

In Jiménez et al (2011), we use a uniquely comprehensive credit register from Spain that, matched with bank and firm relevant information, contains exhaustive loan (bank-firm) level data on all outstanding business loan contracts at a quarterly frequency since 1984:IV, and loan application information at the bank-firm level at a monthly frequency since 2002:02.

Our identification strategy consists of three crucial components:

1. Interacting the overnight interest rate with bank capital (the main theory-based measure of bank agency problems) and a firm credit-risk measure
2. Accounting fully for both observed and unobserved time-varying bank and firm heterogeneity by saturating the specifications with time*bank and time*firm fixed effects (at a quarterly or monthly frequency), and when possible, also controlling for unobserved heterogeneity in bank-firm matching with bank*firm fixed effects and time-varying bank-firm characteristics (past bank-firm credit volume for example).
3. Including in all key specifications – and concurrent with the short-term rate – also the ten-year government-bond interest rate, in particular in a triple interaction with bank capital and a firm credit risk measure (as in (2)).

Spain offers an ideal setting to employ this identification strategy because it has an exhaustive credit register from the banking supervisor, an economic system dominated by banks and, for the last 22 years, a fairly exogenous monetary policy.

We find the following results for a decrease in the overnight interest rate (even when controlling for changes in the ten-year government-bond interest rate):

1. On the intensive margin, a rate cut induces lowly capitalized banks to expand credit to riskier firms more than highly capitalized banks, where firm credit risk is either measured as having an *ex ante* bad credit history (ie, past doubtful loans) or as facing future credit defaults.
2. On the extensive margin of ended lending, a rate cut has if anything a similar impact, ie, lowly capitalized banks end credit to riskier firms less often than highly capitalized banks.
3. On the extensive margin of new lending, a rate cut leads lower-capitalized banks to more likely grant loans to applicants with a worse credit history, and to grant them larger loans or loans with a longer maturity. A decrease in the long-term rate has a much smaller or no such effects on bank risk-taking (on all margins of lending).

Our results in Jiménez et al (2011) suggest that, fully accounting for the credit-demand, firm, and bank balance-sheet channels, monetary policy affects the composition of credit supply. A lower monetary-policy rate spurs bank risk-taking. Suggestive of *excessive* risk-taking are their findings that risk-taking occurs especially at banks with less capital at stake, ie, those afflicted by agency problems, and that credit risk-taking is combined with vigorous liquidity risk-taking (increase in long-term lending to high credit risk borrowers) even when controlling for a long-term interest rate.

In work with Vasso Ioannidou, we also investigate the impact of monetary policy on the risk-taking by banks (Ioannidou et al 2009). This study focuses on the pricing of the risk banks take in Bolivia (relying on a different and complementary identification strategy to Jiménez, et al 2011 and studying data from a developing country). Examining the credit register from Bolivia from 1999 to 2003, we find that, when the US federal-funds rate decreases, bank credit risk increases while loan spreads drop (the Bolivian economy is largely dollarised and most loans are dollar-denominated making the federal-funds rate the appropriate but exogenously determined monetary-policy rate). The latter result is again suggestive of excessive bank risk-taking following decreases in the monetary-policy rate. Hence, despite using very different methodologies, and credit registers covering different countries, time periods, and monetary policy regimes, both papers find strikingly consistent results.

There are a number of natural extensions to these studies. Our focus on the impact of monetary policy on individual loan granting overlooks the correlations between borrower risk and the impact on each individual bank's portfolio or the correlations between all the banks' portfolios and the resulting systemic-risk impact of monetary policy. In addition, both studies focus on the effects of monetary policy on the composition of credit supply in only one dimension, ie, firm risk. Industry affiliation or portfolio distribution between mortgages, consumer loans and business loans for example may also change. Given the intensity of agency problems, social costs and externalities in banking, banks' risk-taking – and other compositional changes of their credit supply for that matter – can be expected to directly impact future financial stability and economic growth. We plan to broach all such extensions in future work.

Disclaimer: Any views expressed are only those of the authors and should not be attributed to the Banco de España, the European Central Bank, or the Eurosystem.

References

Acharya, Viral V and Hassan Naqvi (2010) "The Seeds of a Crisis: A Theory of Bank Liquidity and Risk-taking over the Business Cycle", mimeo, New York University.

Acharya, Viral V and Matthew Richardson (2010) *Restoring Financial Stability: How to Repair a Failed System*. New York: John Wiley & Sons.

Adrian, Tobias and Hyun Song Shin (2010) "Financial Intermediaries and Monetary Economics", in Friedman, Benjamin M and Michael Woodford (eds), *Handbook of Monetary Economics*. New York: Elsevier.

Allen, Franklin and Douglas Gale (2004) "Asset Price Bubbles and Monetary Policy", in Desai, Meghnad and Yahia Said (eds), *Global Governance and Financial Crises*. London: Routledge.

Allen, Franklin and Douglas Gale (2007) *Understanding Financial Crises*. New York: Oxford University Press.

Bernanke, Ben S and Alan S Blinder (1992) "The Federal Funds Rate and the Channels of Monetary Transmission", *American Economic Review* 82: 901-921.

Bernanke, Ben S, Mark Gertler, and Simon Gilchrist (1996) "The Financial Accelerator and the Flight to Quality", *Review of Economics and Statistics* 78: 1-15.

Blanchard, Olivier (2008) "The State of Macro", Working Paper 14259, National Bureau for Economic Research.

Borio, Claudio and Haibin Zhu (2008) "Capital Regulation, Risk-taking and Monetary Policy: A Missing Link in the Transmission Mechanism", Working Paper 268, Bank for International Settlements.

Calomiris, Charles W (2009) "The Subprime Turmoil: What's Old, What's New and What's Next?", *Journal of Structured Finance* 15: 6-52.

De Nicolò, Gianni, Giovanni Dell'Ariccia, Luc Laeven, and Fabian Valencia (2010) "Monetary Policy and Bank Risk-taking," mimeo, International Monetary Fund.

Den Haan, Wouter J, Steven Sumner, and Guy Yamashiro (2007) "Bank Loan Portfolios and the Monetary Transmission Mechanism", *Journal of Monetary Economics* 54: 904-924.

Diamond, Douglas W and Raghuram G Rajan (2006) "Money in a Theory of Banking", *American Economic Review* 96: 30-53.

Diamond, Douglas W and Raghuram G Rajan (forthcoming) "Fear of Fire Sales, Illiquidity Seeking, and Credit Freezes", *Quarterly Journal of Economics* 126.

Diamond, Douglas W and Raghuram G Rajan (2011a) "Illiquid Banks, Financial Stability, and Interest Rate Policy", mimeo, Booth School of Business.

Gennaioli, Nicola, Andrei Shleifer, and Robert Vishny (2011) "A Model of Shadow Banking", mimeo, CREI.

Gertler, Mark and Simon Gilchrist (1994) "Monetary Policy, Business Cycles, and the Behavior of Small Manufacturing Firms", *Quarterly Journal of Economics* 109: 309-340.

Giavazzi, Francesco and Alberto Giovannini (2010) "The Low-Interest-Rate Trap", VoxEU.org, 19 June.

Ioannidou, Vasso P, Steven Ongena, and José-Luis Peydró (2009) "Monetary Policy, Risk-taking and Pricing: Evidence from a Quasi-Natural Experiment", mimeo, CentER - Tilburg University / European Central Bank.

Jiménez, Gabriel, Steven Ongena, José-Luis Peydró, and Jesús Saurina (forthcoming) "Credit Supply and Monetary Policy: Identifying the Bank Balance-Sheet Channel with Loan Applications", *American Economic Review*.

Jiménez, Gabriel, Steven Ongena, José-Luis Peydró, and Jesús Saurina, (2011), "Hazardous Times for Monetary Policy: What Do Twenty-Three Million Bank Loans Say about the Effects of Monetary Policy on Credit Risk-taking?", mimeo, Bank of Spain.

Kashyap, Anil K and Jeremy C Stein (2000) "What Do A Million Observations on Banks Say About the Transmission of Monetary Policy?", *American Economic Review* 90: 407-428.

Maddaloni, Angela and Jose-Luis Peydró (2011) "Bank Risk-taking, Securitization, Supervision, and Low Interest Rates: Evidence from Euro-area and US Lending Standards", Review of Financial Studies 24: 2121-2165.

Mian, Atif and Amir Sufi (2009) "The Consequences of Mortgage Credit Expansion: Evidence from the US Mortgage Default Crisis", *Quarterly Journal of Economics* 124: 1449-1496.

Rajan, Raghuram G (2006) "Has Finance Made the World Riskier?", *European Financial Management* 12: 499-533.

Rajan, Raghuram G (2010) *Fault Lines*. Princeton NJ: Princeton University Press.

Reinhart, Carmen M and Kenneth S Rogoff (2010) *This Time is Different: Eight Centuries of Financial Folly*. Princeton NJ: Princeton University Press.

Stiglitz, Joseph E and Bruce Greenwald (2003) *Towards a New Paradigm in Monetary Economics*. Cambridge: Cambridge University Press.

Taylor, John (2007) "Housing and Monetary Policy", paper presented at a symposium sponsored by the Federal Reserve Bank of Kansas City at Jackson Hole WY, Federal Reserve Bank of Kansas City.

von Hagen, Jürgen and Tai-Kuang Ho (2007) "Money Market Pressure and the Determinants of Banking Crises", *Journal of Money, Credit and Banking* 39: 1037-1066.

About the author

Steven Ongena is a Professor in Empirical Banking at CentER - Tilburg University in the Netherlands and a CEPR Research Fellow in financial economics. His research interests include firm-bank relationships, bank mergers and acquisitions, and financial systems.

José-Luis Peydró is an Associate Professor (with Tenure) at Universitat Pompeu Fabra, an Affiliate Professor at Barcelona GSE, and an Economist in the European Central Bank. His research interests are in banking, macro-prudential policy, financial crises, monetary policy, international finance and macro-finance.

Destabilising market forces and the structure of banks going forward

Arnoud W.A. Boot
University of Amsterdam and CEPR

The financial sector has become increasingly complex in terms of its speed and interconnectedness. This chapter says that market discipline won't stabilise financial markets, and complexity makes regulating markets more difficult. It advocates substantial intervention in order to restructure the banking industry, address institutional complexity, and correct misaligned incentives.

The financial services sector has gone through unprecedented turmoil in the last few years. We see fundamental forces that have affected the stability of financial institutions. In particular, information technology has led to an enormous proliferation of financial markets, but also opened up the banks' balance sheets by enhancing the marketability of their assets. As a matter of fact, a fundamental feature of recent financial innovations – securitisation, for example – is that they are often aimed at augmenting marketability. Such marketability can augment diversification opportunities, but it also creates systemic risk via herding behaviour and interconnectedness.

More fundamentally, when markets exist for all kinds of real and financial assets of a firm, a firm can more easily change the direction of its strategy. This might be good, but could also lead to more impulsive decision making and possibly herding. The latter refers to the tendency to follow current fads. In banking, herding is particularly worrisome because it could create systemic risk – meaning, when all institutions make the same bets, risk exposures become more highly correlated and a simultaneous failure of institutions might become more likely.

We see the complexity of the financial sector (the fluid nature of the sector and difficulties in timely intervention by supervisors) and the systemic risk that has mushroomed as the two key issues that need to be addressed. Endogenous developments in the industry itself may not lead to less complex institutions. Market discipline – as we will argue next – also cannot be expected to be effective. The important question then is how to deal with this complexity. We will argue that imposing structural measures on the business models of banks might be needed to contain possibly destabilising market forces and improve the effectiveness of supervision.

Failure of market discipline adds to destabilising market forces

The increasingly fluid and complex nature of the banking industry – via speed of change, interconnectedness, and the presence of large and complex institutions – has motivated some to point to the importance of market discipline in banking as a supplement to regulatory and supervisory controls. But can we expect that markets will control the behaviour of financial institutions? We see a paradox in the notion of market discipline. The opportunistic behaviour that we pointed at is driven by banks engaging in particular financial market-driven strategies. Those strategies are heavily promoted by momentum in the financial markets that typically mushrooms in euphoric times. Financial markets more or less encourage banks to (opportunistically) exploit them.

But now the paradox. In the way we have formulated the argument, financial markets that are supposed to engage in market discipline are momentum-driven, and hence encourage banks to engage in specific activities. How then can we expect these same markets to impose market discipline? It appears to us that market discipline is not present when banks follow financial market-inspired strategies. Things are even worse because the correlation in strategies between financial institutions will then be high because all see the same opportunities and hence we see herding behaviour. Systemic risk would be enormous and not checked by market discipline.

It follows from this analysis that, from a macroprudential view (ie a system-wide view), market discipline is not effective. This supports Flannery's (2009) analysis that in the summer of 2007 neither share prices nor CDS spreads provided information about pending problems. We tend to conclude that market discipline might more readily work for idiosyncratic risk choices of an individual financial institution (ie across institutions) than for the choices of the sector as a whole. In the financial sector with the correlated strategies induced by momentum in financial markets, market discipline seems ineffective.

Complexity does not help: Forces towards scale and scope (and complexity)

With market discipline being ineffective, and complexity (speed of change and interconnectedness) complicating the effectiveness of regulation and supervision, the question is how to improve control over financial institutions. Can it be expected that the structure of banks becomes simpler? While the current statements in the industry might suggest that institutions 'go back to basics', ie reduce organizational complexity, focus, and simplify product offerings (KPMG 2011), we expect that size will continue to be a driver in the industry.

Whether size really offers scale or scope economies is a totally different question. Research on this remains rather inconclusive, or in the words of Richardson, Smith and Walter (2011): "Indeed, the recent studies mirror the findings [...] some 15 years earlier [...] there was no predominance of evidence either for or against economies of scale in the financial sector." But banks might benefit from the protection that size gives. That is, by going for size banks might capitalize on too-big-to-fail, or rather too-interconnected-to-fail, concerns.

Dealing with complexity

From a regulator's perspective, complexity worsens externalities that one might want to contain. Complexity may also put bank supervisors in a dependent position; eg how is timely intervention possible if the complexity of the institution cannot be grasped by supervisors? And a complex financial institution may have many linkages with the financial system at large that are difficult to discern. This may augment concerns about banks being too big, or rather too interconnected, to fail.

One is tempted to conclude that one way of dealing with the complexity is to disentangle activities and put them in separate legal structures ('subsidiaries'). Those subsidiaries could deal on an arms-length basis with each other, with each being adequately capitalized without recourse to each other. This would resemble the non-operating holding company structure that the OECD has promoted in some studies (Blundell-Wignall et al 2009). With such a structure supervisors could possibly more easily (and more quickly) target, ie rescue, systemically important parts of a financial institution in case of distress; other parts could be sold or dismantled.

One could also choose a more radical approach and force a bank to break up or limit its range of activities. Actually, the UK government's Independent Commission on Banking, the Vickers Committee, advocates some structural remedies, particularly 'ring-fencing' the more locally oriented retail-banking operations. In terms of actually implementing new policies, the US appears to be in the lead with the Volcker Rule (part of the Dodd-Frank Act) that seeks to prohibit the involvement of banks in proprietary trading, and limits their investments and sponsorship in hedge funds, private equity and derivative activities.

We see the safeguarding of core-commercial banking functions (like the payment system) and the improvement of possibilities for timely intervention as key public policy objectives. From a policy perspective it is then hard to defend the desirability of very complex institutions considering the difficulty of timely intervention in such institutions. And more limited commercial banking institutions without much exposure to the financial markets and primarily financed by deposits (contrary to less stable wholesale financing) might be better at safeguarding core-commercial banking functions.

What to do?

We do not believe that it is sufficient to only introduce behavioural measures like higher capital requirements. These are undoubtedly needed, including also more system- and cyclical-oriented measures focusing on externalities and interlinkages, but they do little to address the complexity of institutions and the misalignment between market forces and prudential concerns. Instructive in this regard are the counterproductive incentives that higher capital requirements might induce, eg banks might choose to increase their risk exposure following higher capital requirements in order to preserve a high return on equity over this broader capital base (but note, return on equity does not measure nor control for risk and is therefore not the right measure to look at[1]).

We believe that heavy-handed intervention in the structure of the banking industry – possibly building on the work of the OECD, Volcker Rule and the ring-fencing advocated by the UK Independent Committee on Banking – is an inevitable part of the restructuring of the industry. It could address complexity but also help in containing market forces that might run orthogonal to what prudential concerns would dictate – as the insights on market discipline suggest. How to precisely shape the structural measures is an open issue. All proposals currently on the table can be criticized. But safeguarding essential public infrastructure is a laudable objective, and the structure needs to be such that supervisors can have control. The proposals by the UK Independent Committee on Banking seem consistent with this and thus deserve support. This does not mean that

1 Obviously, corporate finance theory tells us that the cost of capital of a bank is not fixed (this is in corporate finance a risk-dependent measure). Return on equity (ROE) is a measure that is not risk-adjusted. It therefore cannot be that maximizing ROE is value-maximizing. Doing as if the cost of capital of a bank is fixed at a high level might induce banks to engage in excessive risk-taking.

such a solution is sufficient. The interlinkages between the ringfenced parts and the rest, and the way the rest operate, need to be focused on as well. We do not believe that there are simple remedies, but we are convinced that we need to find new 'fixed points' in the financial system; not everything can be fluid.

References

Blundell-Wignall, A, G Wehinger, and P Slovik (2009), "The Elephant in the Room: The Need to Deal with What Banks Do", *Financial Market Trends*, 2009(2): 1-26.

Flannery, MJ (2009), "Market Discipline in Bank Supervision", in Berger, AN, P. Molyneux, and JOS Wilson (eds),*The Oxford Handbook of Banking*. Oxford: Oxford University Press.

KPMG (2011), "UK Banks: Performance Benchmarking Report. Full Year Results 2010".

Richardson, M, RC Smith and I Walter (2011), "Large Banks and the Volcker Rule", in Acharya, VV, TF Cooley, MP Richardson, and I Walter (eds), *Regulating Wall Street: The Dodd-Frank Act and the New Architecture of Global Finance*. Hoboken NJ: Wiley.

About the author

Arnoud Boot is Professor of Corporate Finance and Financial Markets at the University of Amsterdam and director of the Amsterdam Center for Law & Economics (ACLE). He is a member of the Advisory Scientific Committee of the ESRB (European Systemic Risk Council), the Dutch Social Economic Council (SER) and the Bank Council of the Dutch Central Bank (DNB). He is also Research Fellow at the Centre for Economic Policy Research.

Ring-fencing is good, but no panacea

Viral V. Acharya
Stern School of Business, NYU and CEPR

The Vickers Commission recommends separating commercial and non-commercial banking activities in order to protect core financial functions from riskier activities. This chapter warns that such ring-fencing may fail because there are still incentive problems in traditional banking activities. The accompanying risk-weighted capital requirement recommendations will address this only if we do a better job of measuring risks.

The recent report issued by the UK's Independent Commission on Banking, chaired by Sir John Vickers, provided recommendations on capital requirements and contained a proposal to ring fence banks – in particular, their retail versus investment activities. I view ring-fencing as potentially useful but argue that the more important question is whether the risk weights in current Basel capital requirements are appropriate.

The backdrop of the Vickers Commission report is that countries such as the UK, Sweden, and some others, where the financial sectors are rather large compared to the size of the countries, are getting increasingly concerned about facing the kind of banking crises that we faced in 2008. The risks of a double-dip recession and a slowdown in global growth have increased given the tentative recovery in the US and the sovereign debt problems in Europe. Hence, some countries are trying for something more substantial in financial sector reforms than what the Basel III reforms are offering.

Sweden has gone for relatively high levels of capital requirements. The UK is unique in considering the ring-fencing solution, which involves trying to separate the riskier parts of banking activities (mainly investment banking and proprietary trading) from what are considered the core or 'plumbing' aspects, such as payment and settlement systems, deposits, interbank markets, and bank lending, which in turn are primarily centered in the commercial banking activities. The Vickers report concludes that the risks that the commercial banking system, which is at the centre of the plumbing, faces from non-commercial banking activities are serious enough in the current economic climate that we ought to think about some ring-fencing of this sort.

While ring-fencing seems reasonable when viewed in this manner, there is an important risk that any ring-fencing operation will have to worry about – ring-fencing in and of itself is not a panacea. In particular, banks may be encouraged to take greater risks with activities that are inside the fence, such as mortgages, corporate loans, and personal loans.

Ring-fencing ensures that if risks hit the non-commercial banking aspects or if some mistakes happen there – maybe the current UBS trading loss is an example – then the risks will not directly spill over into the commercial banking aspects. However, if there are risk-taking incentives inherent within the commercial banking arm as well – and if what we saw happen during 2003-07 through the trading aspects was just a reflection of that deeper problem – then of course we really would not have solved the real problem. We would have likely just transferred it somewhere else.

Therefore some other fixes are crucial. For instance, it is crucial that a resolution authority be in place globally to wind down in an orderly manner a large, complex financial institution (which even some pure commercial banks are) and ensure that their capital requirements are in sync with the kind of systemic risk that such institutions are undertaking.

In fact, a point in favour of focussing more on improving regulation of the traditional banking aspects is that in the end what really brought down banks and complex organisations in the crisis of 2007-08 was not just the quality of their trading activities. A large part of the portfolios of risky mortgages and mortgage backed securities were held just as straight commercial banking exposures. That is, these risks appeared in their traditional banking mortgage books themselves. Ring-fencing, by itself, would not necessarily have reduced these exposures.

In this regard, it is useful to consider the capital requirements announced in the Vickers report. Banks will be required to hold equity capital of at least 10% of risk weighted assets in the ring fenced business, and both parts of the bank will be required to have total loss absorbing capital of at least 17% to 20%. This seems substantially higher than what Basel III has proposed. The requirements are in fact more in line with the levels of capital requirements that Switzerland has been implementing. The requirements are also somewhat higher than those tentatively discussed in the US, though we are waiting for further clarity on what will be the systemic capital surcharge for systemically important financial institutions in the US under the implementation of the Dodd Frank Act.

The key point is that whatever the capital requirements – 10% and 17% or 18% – it is as a function of risk weighted assets. The fundamental question that has not been put on the table is, are the current risk weights – and the overall framework for determining them – right? In particular, we have very low risk weights on residential mortgage backed securities. What that did was actually *increase* the lending to the residential mortgages as an asset class. Endogenously, therefore, ie, as a response to the capital requirement itself, the residential housing became a systemically important asset class. However, all through the crisis, and even post crisis, we have continued with a relatively attractive risk weight on this asset class – in spite of the fact that the crisis effectively told us that what banks were holding as capital against these assets was not adequate from a resiliency standpoint as far as bank creditors and investors were concerned.

We are in fact facing a similar problem with respect to the sovereign debt holdings of the troubled countries in Europe. Their bonds are being held by banks all over the world, especially in other Eurozone countries. These bond-holdings have so far, as long as they are in banking books of banks (and hence, not ring-fenced), not received substantial haircuts in regulatory capital assessments. In turn, banks have not been asked to raise substantial capital against them (though we might finally see some pan-European bank recapitalization plan). Investors are, however, treating these bond-holdings as risky so that regulatory bank capital and market values of bank capital are completely out of sync.

Therefore, while increasing the level of capital under some circumstances makes sense, we ought to ask whether the risk weights that go into calculating the required capital are right or not, because otherwise we might be raising capital to 20% of risk-weighted assets but the risk might have been poorly calculated. Worse, banks have incentives precisely to hold those assets whose regulatory risk weights are lowest (or most poorly calculated) relative to the implied market-required weights (which can be implied from market valuations, for example).

The second point is that often the current level of capital held by an institution is not as important as what its level of capital is going to be if it is hit by a substantial crisis. This issue ties in with my first point about risk weights. Today, most regulators who are considering subjecting the banking system to stress scenarios would consider as a stress scenario a substantial haircut on the sovereign debt holdings of some of the peripheral countries in Europe, but treat all others as essentially riskless. Recent moves in the Eurozone countries' credit risk have shown that bank recapitalization will put sovereign balance sheets under stress, even in the case of relatively stronger sovereign balance sheets. Now, if banks are charged zero risk weight on bond-holdings of these countries, then it is clear that the levels of capitalization required by the stress tests are never going to be adequate for any future stress on expected recoveries and valuations of bonds of these sovereigns.

In contrast, a capital requirement that deals adequately with future systemic risk should be based on bank losses in stress scenarios, where the scenarios consider losses in assets that have not yet experienced any significant risk revisions. Such a requirement has the feature of charging higher risk weights to those assets that are going to lose under future stress scenarios. Such capital requirements can be conceptually formalized as well as empirically implemented, as explained in another piece in this book ("How to Set

Capital Requirements in a Systemically Risky World" by Viral V Acharya and Matthew Richardson) which explains how NYU Systemic Risk Rankings are implemented.

In summary, I support the push for higher capital requirements, but I stress that regulators – in Basel, the UK, Switzerland, and the US – all fundamentally need to rethink whether static risk weights, which do not change when the market's risk assessment of an asset class permanently changes, are really the right way to continue.

If we just keep raising capital to risk-weighted asset ratios but we do not improve our measurement of risks in determining the denominator of these ratios, we have a serious problem on hand. We have moved from a credit bubble in one low risk-weight asset class (housing) to another (sovereign bonds) over the past decade and both have resulted in among the worst crises of our times. It is time to change this state of affairs.

Editor's note: This essay is based on a Vox Talks audio interview between the author and Viv Davies recorded on 16 September 2011.

About the author

Viral V. Acharya is Professor of Finance at the New York University Stern School of Business, and Director of the CEPR Financial Economics Programme. His research interests are in the regulation of banks and financial institutions, corporate finance, valuation of corporate debt, and asset pricing with a focus on the effects of cash management and liquidity risk.

The Dodd-Frank Act, systemic risk and capital requirements

Viral V Acharya and **Matthew Richardson**
Stern School of Business, NYU and CEPR; Stern School of Business, NYU

Macroprudential regulation aims to reduce systemic risk by correcting the negative externalities caused by breakdowns in financial intermediation. This chapter describes the shortcomings of the Dodd-Frank legislation as a piece of macroprudential regulation. It says the Act's ex post charges for systemic risk don't internalise the negative externality and its capital requirements may be arbitrary and easily gamed.

The economic theory of regulation is clear. Governments should regulate where there is a market failure. It is a positive outcome from the Dodd-Frank legislation that the Act's primary focus is on the market failure – namely systemic risk – of the recent financial crisis. The negative externality associated with such risk implies that private markets cannot efficiently solve the problem, thus requiring government intervention.

More concretely, current and past financial crises show that systemic risk emerges when aggregate capitalization of the financial sector is low. The intuition is straightforward. When a financial firm's capital is low, it is difficult for that firm to perform financial services; and when capital is low in the aggregate, it is not possible for other financial firms to step into the breach. This breakdown in financial intermediation is the reason severe consequences occur in the broader economy. When a financial firm therefore runs aground during a crisis period, it contributes to this aggregate shortfall, leading to consequences beyond the firm itself. The firm has no incentive to manage the systemic risk.

For the first time, the Act highlights the need for macroprudential regulation, that is, (i) to measure and provide tools for measuring systemic risk (an example being the Office of Financial Research), (ii) to then designate firms, or even sectors (eg money market funds), that pose systemic risk, and (iii) to provide enhanced regulation of such firms and sectors.

While arguably this type of regulation was always in the purview of central banks and regulators, the current crisis has shown the importance of writing it into law. With sufficient progress in both analytics and regulation, we will several years from now have much better data, much more developed processes for dealing systemic risk, and overall a much better understanding of systemic risk.

We believe the benefits of macroprudential regulation outweigh its costs. However, there are two especially worrying outcomes of the Dodd-Frank Act and its implementation. One concerns the *ex ante* rather than *ex post* charges for systemic risk. The second concerns the calculation of capital charges for systemically important financial institutions.

But first, it needs to be pointed out that the Dodd-Frank Act puts a heavy reliance on the creation of an Orderly Liquidation Authority. Resolution is by its nature a balancing act between two forces that (potentially) work against each other. On the one hand, the regulator would like to mitigate moral hazard and bring back market discipline. On the other hand, the regulator would like to manage systemic risk. So how well does Dodd-Frank do in terms of balancing these two forces? From our viewpoint, it does not perform very well.

It seems to us that the Act is for the most part focused on the orderly liquidation of an individual institution and not the system as a whole. Of course, what is unique about a financial firm's failure during a crisis is that it has an impact on the rest of the financial sector and the broader economy.

To put this into perspective, consider Federal Reserve Chairman Ben Bernanke's oft-cited analogy for why bailouts, however distasteful, are sometimes necessary. Bernanke has described a hypothetical neighbour who smokes in bed and, through his carelessness, starts a fire and begins to burn down his house. You could teach him a lesson, Bernanke says, by refusing to call the fire department and letting the house burn to the ground. However, you would risk the fire spreading to other homes. So first you have to put out the fire. Only later should you deal with reform and retribution. This is what we would call legislation prior to Dodd-Frank.

We would argue that you should call the fire department, but instead of saving the neighbour's house, the firefighters stand in protection of your house and those of your other neighbours. If the fire spreads, they are ready to put it out. And by the way, because a fire company is expensive to keep, we will charge all the smokers in the neighborhood the cost. And over time, the neighborhood will have fewer smokers. This is what we mean by balancing moral hazard mitigation and systemic risk management.

Dodd-Frank does not do this. Here is one example. The Act creates wrong incentives by charging ex post rather than *ex ante* for systemic risk. In particular, if firms fail during a crisis and monies cannot be fully recovered from creditors, the surviving systemically important financial institutions must make up the difference *ex post*. This actually increases moral hazard because there is a free-rider problem – prudent firms are asked to pay for the sins of others. It also increases systemic risk in two important ways. First, firms will tend to herd together and a race to the bottom could ensue. Second, this clause is highly procyclical because it requires the surviving firms to provide capital at the worst possible time.

Our second concern relates to recent developments on the macroprudential dimension. The basic thrust of Basel III is higher capital requirements overall – and then, for systemically risky institutions, even higher capital requirements. The criteria for systemic risk are five factors based on size, interconnectedness, lack of substitutability, complexity, and level of global activity. To the extent that the capital requirements for systemically risky firms could increase by 2.5%, one has a terrible feeling that implementation might be very Basel-like and just assign 0.5% to each of these factors. Whether it is risk weights, level of new capital required, how firms are chosen to be systemic, and surcharges on these systemic firms, it all seems somewhat arbitrary and not based on objective criteria. And, for sure, the implementation will be quite coarse and therefore easily gamed.

What we care about is the risk that a firm will falter when other firms are struggling, in other words, the codependence between financial firms. Key factors that go into this measurement are therefore how much leverage a firm has, how correlated its assets in the bad state of nature are, and whether its failure increases the likelihood of other firms failing.

In the following, we provide one such way to think about setting capital requirements in a systemically risky world.

1. **Why are capital requirements so important and why are capital levels cyclical?** When a large part of the financial sector is funded primarily with leverage and is hit by a common shock such as a steep drop in house prices, individual financial firms cannot meet immediate repayments demanded by their creditors. There simply are not enough well-capitalized, or low-leverage, firms in the system to buy other firms' assets, re-intermediate with their borrowers, or lend at reasonable rates and maturities in interbank markets. Capital is thus the lifeblood of the financial system when it is under stress. But that is precisely when capital becomes scarce. Invariably, an aggregate credit crunch and loss of intermediation ensue.

2. **How should capital requirements be designed in good times to prevent and manage this systemic risk that collective under-capitalization of the financial sector can create spillovers to real and household sectors?** A reasonable criterion is to set the capital requirement such that a financial firm should in expectation have enough capital to withstand a full-blown crisis. In other words, $E[E_i|crisis] \geq K_i E[A_i|crisis]$, where E_i is financial firm i's equity, A_i is the firm's total assets (ie, its equity capital plus debt obligations), and $1/K_i$ is the firm's maximum leverage ratio at which it still provides full financial intermediation. For example, in Basel III, the minimum ratio of common equity capital to assets $K_i = 3\%$.

3. **What does this criterion imply for capital requirements?** It is possible to derive that the minimum required capital *today* is $E_{i0} \geq K_i \frac{A_{i0}}{(1-(1-K_i)MES_i)}$ where *MES* is the firm's marginal expected shortfall, defined as its expected percentage loss in equity capital conditional on a financial crisis.

4. **How would this work?** Consider the recent financial crisis. The average return of the worst quartile of performing bank holding companies was -87% versus -17% for the top performing quartile during the crisis. For the 3% minimum, this would translate to a 19.2% capital requirement before the crisis for the more systemic firms (as measured by ex post MES of 87%) and just 3.6% for the less systemic ones (*MES* of 17%). Alternatively, using *ex ante* measures, the NYU Stern risk rankings of the 100 largest financial firms suggest a range of MES from 40% to 75%, implying capital requirements ranging from 5% to 11%.

5. **What are the key implications of this methodology?**

   a. The first is that this capital requirement is fairly simple to interpret and can be calculated in a straightforward manner. What is required is an expectation of a firm's equity capital loss during a financial crisis. One could employ *statistical-based measures of capital losses* of financial firms extrapolated to crisis periods. With a number of our colleagues here at NYU Stern, we have done just that with state-of-the-art time-series techniques. The aforementioned systemic risk rankings of financial firms are provided at *http://vlab.stern.nyu.edu/welcome/risk*. Of some interest, these measures estimated in 2006 and early 2007 load quite closely on the firms that performed poorly during the financial crisis. Or, regulators could estimate a firm's capital losses during adverse times via *stress tests of financial institutions*. Stress tests are conducted routinely by regulators and the estimated percentage losses from these tests could simply be substituted into the above formula for capital requirements. Of course, the regulator would need to impose scenarios that necessarily coincide with financial crises, in other words, much more severe than those employed in stress tests this year both in the US and Europe.

b. The second point is that our risk factor $\left[\frac{1}{1-(1-K)MES}\right]$ is a scaling-up factor on firm's assets, a kind of 'systemic risk weight' that is rather different from the asset-level risk weights set forth in Basel II, and now expanded in III. A strong case can be made that the current crisis was all about large complex financial firms exploiting loopholes in Basel risk weights to make a one-way concentrated bet on residential and commercial mortgages. By attempting to estimate a firm's losses in a bottom-up, granular manner, the Basel risk weights create room for tremendous gaming by the financial sector, and provide incentives to enter into specific spread trades and concentrate risk. In other words, there is a reason why firms loaded up on AAA-rated higher-yielding securities and purchased protection on these securities from AA- or AAA-rated insurance companies like AIG. In contrast, our approach, based on a top-down, market-based systemic measure, incorporates the risk of the underlying assets when we care most, namely during a financial crisis, and is much harder to game.

6. **What are the capital requirements changes under Basel III?** With respect to capital requirements, Basel III effectively increases (with the conservation of capital buffer) capital requirements from 4% to 7%. On top of these requirements, based on a series of firm characteristics related to Basel's systemic risk criteria, these capital requirements can be increased by an amount ranging from 0%-3%. Along with a number of other adjustments, Basel III introduces a new 'simple' leverage ratio as a supplementary measure to risk-based capital which is to be set at 3%. For practical purposes, Basel III continues the risk weights that are tied to credit ratings both within and across asset classes.

7. **Are the changes under Basel III sensible?**

   a. First and foremost, the systemic risk weights seem arbitrary and are not based on objective criteria. Thus, across-the-board higher capital requirements, as are being proposed for systemically important financial institutions, may actually exacerbate the problem. Regulation should not be about more capital per se but about more capital for systemically riskier financial firms.

   b. Second, our methodology makes clear that higher capital requirements resulting from systemic risk do not have to coincide with larger financial institutions. For a variety of reasons, it may well be the case that large financial institutions deserve heightened prudential regulation. But if the criterion is that they need sufficient capital to withstand a crisis, it does not follow that size necessarily is the key factor unless it adversely affects a firm's marginal expected shortfall, ie its performance in a crisis.

   c. Third, it is certainly the case that a bank's return on equity does not map one-to-one with a bank's valuation. A higher return on equity might simply reflect higher leverage on the bank's part, and the benefit of leverage may be arising from the government safety net. Therefore, calling for a higher equity capital requirement may be sensible. That said, there seems to be little economic analysis of what the right level of capital should be.

   d. Finally, whatever is being proposed for the banking sector in terms of capital requirements should have comparable regulation for the shadow banking sector, lest the activities simply be shifted from one part of financial markets to another. The result of such a shift could actually lead to an increase in systemic risk.

About the authors

Viral V. Acharya is Professor of Finance at the New York University Stern School of Business, and Director of the CEPR Financial Economics Programme. His research interests are in the regulation of banks and financial institutions, corporate finance, valuation of corporate debt, and asset pricing with a focus on the effects of cash management and liquidity risk.

Matthew Richardson is the Charles E. Simon Professor of Applied Economics in the Finance Department at the Leonard N. Stern School of Business at New York University. Professor Richardson has done research in many areas of finance, including both theoretical and empirical work.

Bank governance and regulation

Luc Laeven
IMF and CEPR

Recent financial regulatory reforms target banks' risk-taking behaviours without considering their ownership and governance. This chapter argues that bank governance influences how regulations alter banks' incentives. Banks with more powerful owners tend to take more risks, and greater capital requirements actually increase risk-taking in banks with powerful shareholders. Bank regulation should condition on bank governance.

Regulations for banks are being rewritten in response to the global financial crisis. The Basel III framework is being adopted, capital requirements are being increased, and safety nets have expanded in scope and size, all with the aim of making banks safer. These financial reforms and re-regulations, however, ignore bank governance – the ownership of banks and the incentives and conflicts that arise between bank owners and managers. But what if the governance structure of banks is intrinsically linked to bank risk? And what if bank governance interacts with regulation to shape bank stability?

This emphasis on using official regulations to induce sound banking while ignoring the role of bank governance is surprising because standard agency theories suggest that ownership structure influences corporate risk-taking (Jensen and Meckling 1976). This gap is also potentially serious from a policy perspective. The same regulations could have different effects on bank risk-taking depending on the comparative power of shareholders within the ownership structure of each bank. Changes in policies toward bank ownership, such as allowing private equity groups to invest in banks or changing limits on ownership concentration, could have very different effects on bank stability depending on other bank regulations.

Yet research on bank risk-taking typically does not incorporate information on each bank's ownership structure. In an exception, Saunders et al (1990) find that owner-controlled banks exhibit higher risk-taking behaviour than banks controlled by managers with small shareholdings. They do not, however, analyse whether ownership structure and regulations jointly shape bank risk-taking, or whether their results generalise beyond the United States to countries with distinct laws and regulations.

Banks naturally take more risk than is optimal for society because their shareholders are subject to limited liability. As in any limited liability firm, diversified owners have incentives to increase bank risk after collecting funds from bondholders and depositors (Galai and Masulis 1976). However, the ability of bank shareholders to maximise their equity value by increasing risk depends in part on the preferences of the bank's managers and on the constraints imposed on bank risk-taking by bank regulation and the regulators that enforce such regulation (Buser et al 1981).

The risk-taking incentives of bank managers will depend on the degree to which their interests are linked to those of value-maximising stockholders. Managers with bank-specific human capital skills and private benefits of control tend to advocate less risk-taking than stockholders without those skills and benefits (Jensen and Meckling 1976, Demsetz and Lehn 1985, John et al 2008). From this perspective, banks with an ownership structure that empowers diversified owners take on more risk than banks with owners who play a more subdued governance role. Of course, to the extent that the manager has a large equity stake in the bank or holds stock options, this would enhance his or her risk-taking incentives by enticing them with potentially large rewards for high-return investments. In practice, however, bank managers often do not hold much bank stock, placing them at odds with diversified bank owners in their views on risk-taking.

To complicate matters further, the effectiveness of bank regulation to curtail bank risk-taking will also depend on the incentives of the bank regulators that enforce such regulations. With self-interested bank regulators that have private benefits or concerns (such as reputational concerns from intervening in banks) or can be captured by industry, regulation to constrain bank risk-taking may be muted.

Theory also predicts that regulations influence the risk-taking incentives of diversified owners differently from those of debt holders and non-shareholder managers. For example, deposit insurance intensifies the ability and incentives of stockholders to increase risk (Merton 1977, Keeley 1990). The impetus for greater risk-taking generated by deposit insurance operates on owners, not necessarily on non-shareholder managers. As a second example, consider capital regulations. One goal of capital regulations is to reduce the risk-taking incentives of owners by forcing owners to place more of their personal wealth at risk in the bank (Kim and Santomero 1994). Capital regulations need not reduce the risk-taking incentives of influential owners, however. Specifically, although capital regulations might induce the bank to raise capital, they might not force influential owners to invest more of their wealth in the bank. Furthermore, capital regulations might increase risk-taking. Owners might compensate for the loss of utility from more stringent capital requirements by selecting a riskier investment portfolio (Gale 2010), intensifying conflicts between owners and managers over bank risk-taking. As a final example, many countries attempt to reduce bank risk by restricting banks from engaging in non-lending activities, such as securities and insurance underwriting. As with capital requirements, however, these activity restrictions could reduce the utility of owning a bank, intensifying the risk-taking incentives of owners relative to managers. Thus, the impact of regulations on risk depends on the comparative influence of owners within the governance structure of each bank.

While banking theory suggests that bank regulations affect the risk-taking incentives of owners differently from those of managers, corporate governance theory suggests that ownership structure affects the ability of owners to influence risk. As argued by Shleifer and Vishny (1986), shareholders with larger voting and cash-flow rights have correspondingly greater power and incentives to shape corporate behaviour than smaller owners. From this perspective, ownership structure influences the ability of owners to alter bank risk in response both to standard risk-shifting incentives and to incentives created by official regulations.

Taken together, these theories predict that diversified owners have stronger incentives to increase risk than non-shareholder managers, so banks with powerful, diversified owners tend to be riskier than widely held banks, holding other factors constant. They also predict that bank regulations affect the risk-taking incentives of owners differently from managers, so the actual impact of regulations on risk-taking depends on the comparative power of shareholders relative to managers within each bank's corporate governance structure.

In a recent paper (Laeven and Levine 2009), we make a first attempt to test how national regulations interact with a bank's private governance structure to determine its risk-taking behaviour. We find that banks with more powerful owners (as measured by the size of their shareholdings) tend to take greater risks. This supports arguments predicting that equity holders have stronger incentives to increase risk than non-shareholding managers and debt holders, and that owners with substantial cash flows have the power and incentives to induce the bank's managers to increase risk-taking.

Furthermore, the impact of bank regulations on bank risk depends critically on each bank's ownership structure such that the relation between regulation and bank risk can change sign depending on ownership structure. For example, the results suggest that deposit insurance is only associated with an increase in risk when the bank has a large equity holder with sufficient power to act on the additional risk-taking incentives created by deposit insurance. The data also suggest that owners seek to compensate for the loss in value of owning a bank from capital regulations by increasing bank risk. Stricter capital regulations are associated with greater risk when the bank has a sufficiently powerful owner, but stricter capital regulations have the opposite effect in widely held banks. Ignoring bank governance leads to incomplete and sometimes erroneous conclusions about the impact of bank regulations on bank risk-taking.

These findings have important policy implications. They question the current approach to bank supervision and regulation that relies on internationally established capital regulations and supervisory practices. Instead, private governance mechanisms exert a powerful influence over bank risking and the same official regulation has different effects on bank risk-taking depending on the bank's governance structure. Since governance structures differ systematically across countries, bank regulations must be custom-designed and adapted as financial governance systems evolve. Regulations should be geared toward creating sound incentives for owners, managers, and debt holders, not toward harmonising national regulations across economies with very different governance structures.

Naturally, regulations will shape the future of banking. It is not too late for bank regulation to condition on bank governance, and for supervision with limited resources to make the enforcement of regulation a function of a bank's governance structure. For example, supervisors could allocate a disproportionate amount of their resources to supervising those banks that corporate governance theory would indicate are intrinsically more inclined to take risk, such as owner-controlled banks and/or banks with concentrated ownership. More generally, the risk-taking of banks will depend on the underlying incentives and preferences of the banks managers and owners, including their ownership and wealth concentration in the bank.

Finally, it is important to recognise that the risk-shifting incentives of banks arising from limited liability would be significantly reduced if bank owners would be subject to extended liability – for example, through double liability which holds each shareholder liable to the amount of the par value of the shares held by him, in addition to the amount invested in such shares (Esty 1998). While holding shareholders liable for a portion of the bank's debts after insolvency would significantly increase the cost of capital and therefore reduce the lending capacity of banks with potentially negative ramifications for growth, it would create safer banks and therefore should not easily be discarded as a policy option to enhance financial stability.

Disclaimer: While the author of this chapter is a staff member of the International Monetary Fund, the views expressed herein are those of the author and should not be attributed to the IMF, its Executive Board, or its management.

References

Buser, S, A Chen, and E Kane (1981) "Federal Deposit Insurance, Regulatory Policy, and Optimal Bank Capital," *Journal of Finance* 36, 51-60.

Demsetz, H and K Lehn (1985) "The Structure of Corporate Ownership: Causes and Consequences," *Journal of Political Economy* 93, 1155-1177.

Esty, B (1998) "The Impact of Contingent Liability on Commercial Bank Risk-taking," *Journal of Financial Economics* 47, 189-218.

Galai, D and R Masulis (1976) "The Option Pricing Model and the Risk Factor of Stock," *Journal of Financial Economics* 3, 53-81.

Gale, D (2010) "Capital Regulation and Risk Sharing," *International Journal of Central Banking* 23, 187-204.

Jensen, M and W Meckling (1976) "Theory of the Firm: Managerial Behaviour, Agency Costs, and Ownership Structure," *Journal of Financial Economics* 3, 305-360.

John, K, L Litov and B Yeung (2008) "Corporate Governance and Managerial Risk Taking: Theory and Evidence," *Journal of Finance* 63, 1679-1728.

Keeley, M (1990) "Deposit Insurance, Risk, and Market Power in Banking," *American Economic Review* 80, 1183-1200.

Kim, D and A Santomero (1994) "Risk in Banking and Capital Regulation," *Journal of Finance* 43, 1219-1233.

Laeven, L and R Levine (2009) "Bank Governance, Regulation, and Risk-Taking," *Journal of Financial Economics* 93, 259-275.

Merton, R (1977) "An Analytic Derivation of the Cost of Deposit Insurance and Loan Guarantees: An Application of Modern Option Pricing Theory," *Journal of Banking and Finance* 1, 3-11.

Saunders, A, E Strock, and NG Travlos (1990) "Ownership Structure, Deregulation, and Bank Risk Taking", *Journal of Finance* 45, 643-654.

Shleifer, A and R Vishny (1986) "Large Shareholders and Corporate Control," *Journal of Political Economy* 94, 461-488.

About the author

Luc Laeven is Deputy Division Chief in the Research Department of the International Monetary Fund, Full Professor of Finance at CentER, Tilburg University and a CEPR Research Fellow. Prior to this, he was a Senior Economist at the World Bank. His research focuses on international banking and corporate finance.

Systemic liquidity risk: A European approach

Enrico Perotti
University of Amsterdam and CEPR

How should financial regulators address problems stemming from liquidity risk? This chapter argues that the liquidity coverage and net funding ratios proposed for Basel III are economically and politically impractical. It recommends using those ratios as long-term targets while imposing 'prudential risk surcharges' on deviations from the targets.

The repeated bursts of financial distress in Europe in 2010-11 reflect vulnerabilities built up in the previous decade and are germane to the roots of the credit crisis.

Abundant global liquidity relaxed funding constraints for banks and their borrowers, whether governments, firms, or consumers. Private and public debt grew faster than domestic savings as they were funded externally, by wholesale funding. Such funding is cheap because it is short-term, uninsured, and uninformed, and therefore prone to runs. This classic problem of 'hot money' for developing countries has now reached developed economies, since they have become large net borrowers.

Credit grew fastest in the Eurozone's periphery, where the stability induced by the euro eased historical concerns about private productivity or fiscal laxness. Banks abandoned organic growth on local business credit, and escalated lending to unsustainable real estate booms and excess public consumption. As this balance-sheet expansion was built on a very unstable funding structure, Eurozone banks are now visibly over-reliant on jittery wholesale credit flows.

A radical new architecture is needed to restore proper credit incentives and strengthen resilience, moving banks away from a failed business model. Central to this transformation is to steer a desirable structure of bank funding. A banking system based on more stable funding (retail deposits and informed, long-term investors) would also promote a focus on local business credit opportunities, moving away from the oversized carry trades, investing in risky global assets and funding it with unstable global liquidity.

Prudential control of liquidity risk under Basel III

In the ongoing regulatory reform, attention has focused on raising capital ratios. Under Basel II, capital charges were inadequate, relying excessively on credit ratings and industry modelling. The new proposals are a large improvement, and a broad agreement has now been reached.

Basel III also seeks to address liquidity risk, recognized as the biggest gap in Basel II. Understanding bank equity is, unfortunately, much easier than understanding liquidity risk. After all, even a bank with a 10% adjusted-capital ratio usually has a 95/96% debt-to-assets ratio, after removing capital discounts for safe assets (such as all Eurozone sovereign debt!). So the key question is – how can we control refinancing risk for 95% of bank funding, given that banks are tempted to raise cheap, short-term funding and rely on central bank rescues should a run occur?

Academic opinion agrees that unstable funding imposes a negative risk externality. Both risk charges and mandatory ratios have been proposed to contain liquidity risk buildup (Perotti and Suarez 2009; Acharya, Khrishnamurti and Perotti 2011). However, the Basel III proposals have been cast solely in terms of ratios.

Two standards have been introduced:

- Liquidity coverage ratios: buffers of liquid assets as a fraction of less stable funding.
- Net funding ratios: quantitative limits to short-term funding.

While very tight levels of such ratios can ensure stability, this approach is too narrow.

The ratios are:

- Too rigid. As they are fixed, they need to be set tight enough to be adequate all the time. As a result they are easily characterised as very expensive, and create massive resistance.
- Not countercyclical. In fact, buffers are clearly procyclical (Perotti and Suarez 2010). The reason is that buffers discourage aggregate net liquidity risk only if they are costly. But in good times, the wholesale funding spread for banks is minimal (it was basically zero in 2004-07), while it jumps in a crisis. So unstable funding exposure is not discouraged, and net exposure will be the same as without buffers. Even *ex post*, buffers are clearly insufficient to contain systemic runs.
- Very distortionary (relative to charges). They penalise the more efficient lenders, which will be rigidly constrained. This is analogous to the reason why quotas are usually less efficient than tariffs.

On the positive side, quantity limits on unstable funding are a robust solution when banks are very undercapitalised. In that case, many banks are too prone to gambling to rely on charges alone. Yet in practice, when banks' capital ratios are weak, authorities are forced to offer extensive liquidity support, and to abandon tight standards. So ratios would work because they are very constraining, but will not be used precisely *because* they are.

It is extraordinary that contrary to a broad academic consensus, central banks' lists of macroprudential tools do not consider alternatives to ratios, even though the approach is at serious risk of derailment.

- The ratios have been successfully portrayed as very tight (as perhaps they need to be since they are set once and for all), and unaffordable in the current climate. The US regulators are currently under heavy lobbying pressure, and given the political climate, they are unlikely to adopt very tight recommendations. Inexplicably, the European Commission has neglected any reference in its CRD4 report to the most critical ratio, the net funding ratio. This omission has caused shock and concern, leading the ECB board to demand an explanation of the Commission's intentions.

- The introduction of these standards has been considerably delayed, with the liquidity coverage ratios not scheduled for some years, and the net funding ratios postponed for much longer. It is extraordinary that no European-level prudential measure will be in place for so many years.
- Even the definition of these ratios has not yet been agreed. The definition of the net funding ratio standards is particularly controversial, and likely to be seriously weakened.
- The buffer measures (liquidity coverage ratios) would require the creation of massive buffers given the current highly mismatched bank funding. These are seen as very costly, and there is an issue of insufficient forms of safe liquid assets to invest in anyway. Under current rules any Eurozone sovereign debt would qualify as a buffer, a curious prudential solution in the midst of the Eurozone sovereign debt crisis.

A key strategic choice

How, then, can regulators introduce prudential measures on liquidity risk that will be effective but not too onerous? The measures must also be introduced earlier than 2019 without disruption to be politically feasible.

A concrete solution, based on broad academic consensus, would be as follows.

Central banks have, during two years of Basel III negotiation, defined desirable liquidity positions in terms of standard ratios. These may be introduced as long-term targets, next to less demanding standards to be implemented immediately.

Banks may choose not to comply with the (higher) desirable standards because of individual circumstances or business model choices. In that case, they would be charged ‘prudential risk surcharges’ on the difference between the desirable and the actual ratios.

Risk charges may start quite low, certainly in a confidence crisis.

These fees would not reflect a direct insurance promise, but reflect the risk externality caused by individual bank strategies on systemic liquidity risk. As such, they represent a non-fiscal form of ‘bank taxation’ which targets risk creation, rather than transaction volumes.

The banks which would be more affected are those with the lowest retail deposits, which have expanded their balance sheets by relying on wholesale funding. This would rebalance the current bias where non-deposit funding is *de facto* insured but evades insurance charges.

The critical feature of ratios is that they may be adjusted countercyclically to stem excess growth of unstable funding. Raising charges would be much easier than adjusting ratios, as they have lower adjustment and disruption costs than quantity adjustments (which as a result are usually delayed for years).

Charges would be less rigid than absolute ratios, enabling individual banks to optimise their adjustment over time. Public disclosure would be limited to aggregate volumes.

The presence of the charges would ensure that:

- Supervisors would be able to monitor on a constant basis the liquidity risk buildup at the individual and system level.
- All banks will be induced to monitor the difference between the desired and current liquidity standing. Up to 2008, most large banks did not have a central tracking of their liquidity exposure.
- Risky strategies could be discouraged in good times without raising interest rates.
- At present, the authority for imposing such charges would lie with national central banks. For some, this step would require legislation.

- Ideally, such a step should be coordinated at the level of the European Union. This would justify an EU directive proposal, ensuring a critical role for the approval process in Brussels for the CRD proposal.
- International coordination of such charges would be desirable though not indispensable. There is no violation of the principle of level playing field, of course, if banks with different risk contributions were charged different amounts. An analogy would be with insurance premia, which may well differ across risk profiles. To illustrate this point further, it is clear that it would have been desirable in 2005-07 for Spain and Ireland to have higher charges on wholesale bank borrowings than, say, Germany, where there was no credit-fuelled real estate boom.
- The natural locus of coordination to set rates would be the ESRB, which would gain an (indirect) macroprudential tool and thus a role. This is consistent with the European Parliament's stated preferences for a more concrete empowerment of the ESRB as a macroprudential regulator.
- Charges would accumulate in reserve funds for general financial-stability purposes.

References

Acharya, Viral, Arvind Krishnamurthy andEnrico Perotti (2011), "A consensus view on liquidity risk," VoxEU.org.

Brunnermeier, Markus, Gary Gorton, and Arvind Krishnamurthy (2011), "Risk Topography", NBER Macroannual 2011.

Perotti, Enrico (2010), "Systemic liquidity risk and bankruptcy exceptions", VoxEU.org.

Perotti, Enrico and Javier Suarez (2011), "The Simple Analytics of Systemic Liquidity Risk Regulation", VoxEU.org.

Perotti, Enrico and Javier Suarez (forthcoming), "A Pigovian Approach to Liquidity Regulation", *International Journal of Central Banking*.

Shin, Hyun Song (2010), "Macroprudential Policies Beyond Basel III", Policy memo.

About the author

Enrico Perotti is Professor of International Finance at the University of Amsterdam and a CEPR Research Fellow. His research is in corporate finance and banking, theory of the firm, political economy of finance, economic and legal innovation, and financial development.

Taxing banks – here we go again!

Thorsten Beck and **Harry Huizinga**
Tilburg University and CEPR

New taxes on the financial sector are likely. The European Commission has proposed a financial transaction tax and a financial activities tax. This chapter evaluates those proposals and identifies other potential taxation mechanisms the EC has overlooked. It says that the proposed measures are poorly suited to curb excessively risky trading and eliminate undertaxation of the financial sector.

For many years, taxation of financial institutions was a topic for specialists, both among tax or public finance economists and among financial economists. The current crisis and the need for large-scale recapitalisations of banks have changed this dramatically, and new taxes on banks now form part of the broader debate on regulatory reform. Over the past three years, several proposals to introduce new financial-sector taxation, in some form or another, have emerged in the political arena, and now the time has come to get specific.

On 28 September 2011, the European Commission published a proposal for a new directive on a common system of financial transaction tax, with an EU-wide tax rate of 0.1% on bond and equity transactions, and of 0.01% on derivative transactions between financial firms.[1]

In its impact assessment study, the European Commission juxtaposes a common financial transaction tax (FTT) with a common financial activities tax (FAT). The FAT

1 See *http://ec.europa.eu/taxation_customs/resources/documents/taxation/other_taxes/financial_sector/com(2011)594_en.pdf*.

would tax the combined profits and wages in the financial sector, as an approximation of its value-added.

Below, we will assess both proposals. However, we maintain that, by presenting us with a horse race between an FTT and an FAT, the European Commission is unduly restricting the debate on appropriate new taxation of the financial sector.

An obvious step towards bringing about appropriate taxation of the financial sector is eliminating the current VAT exemption of most financial services. The current undertaxation of the financial sector resulting from the VAT exemption is mentioned by the European Commission as a main reason to introduce additional taxation of the financial sector. However, if the problem is the current VAT exemption, isn't the right solution to eliminate it?[2] Unfortunately, the European Commission is missing the opportunity to bring the financial sector under full VAT created by the current momentum in favour of more taxation on the financial sector. Instead, the European Commission states that the issue of financial-sector VAT should be solved in the context of a Green Paper on VAT reform, with uncertain timing and outcome.

Unfortunately, by framing the policy choice as between an FTT and an FAT, the Commission is also giving short shrift to the need for a common approach to bank levies in Europe. Bank levies are taxes on a bank's liabilities that generally exclude deposits that are covered by deposit insurance schemes.

Bank levies appropriately follow the 'polluter-pays' principle, as they target the banks – and their high leverage – that are heavily implicated in the recent financial crisis. Bank levies have significant potential to raise revenue and they directly discourage bank leverage, thereby reducing the chance of future bank instability. In sophisticated versions of bank levies, they are targeted at risky bank finance such as short-term wholesale finance, and they may be higher for banks with high leverage, or for banks

2 Huizinga (2002) estimates that bringing financial services under normal VAT would raise around €12.2 billion for the EU15 in 1998, which is equivalent to about 0.15% of GDP

that are systemically important. It is exactly because of these benefits that many individual EU member states are considering or already have in place taxes on bank liabilities.

National, uncoordinated policies regarding bank levies can create competitive distortions in the international banking industry, possibly leading to international bank relocations and international double taxation. Hence, a common EU framework on bank levies would be very helpful, and the failure of the European Commission to publish a proposed directive to coordinate this type of taxation so far is regrettable. In a communication on bank resolution funds published in 2010, the European Commission mentions bank levies as a possible means to finance such funds, but it is unclear whether this thinking will lead to a legislative proposal to coordinate bank levies in the EU.[3] Previously, the IMF (Cotarelli 2010) has come out in favour of either an FAT or bank levies as appropriate ways to impose new taxes on the financial sector, while not favouring an FTT.

Financial transaction tax

Keynes was one of the first prominent proponents of such a tax. In his *General Theory*, he proposed a securities transactions tax to reduce destabilising speculation in equity markets. Tobin suggested a currency transaction tax to throw sand into the overheated gears of the global financial system and to limit speculation by reducing velocity and volume of transactions (Tobin 1978). More recently, its considerable revenue potentials have also come into view. Many economists – including Nobel Prize winners like Paul Krugman and Joseph Stiglitz – have backed the tax. While many proponents have grown uneasy with its anti-speculation merits, they rather focus on the revenue aspect and emphasise that even a relatively low tax rate on a broad range of financial transactions would raise a large volume of revenue, with little distortion of capital flows. Even

3 See *http://ec.europa.eu/internal_market/bank/docs/crisis-management/funds/com2010_254_en.pdf*.

advocates of such a tax, however, recognise that implementing such a tax would require significant international coordination since those taxed would seek to escape the tax by moving activity to another country.

As pointed out by many economists, transaction taxes are too crude an instrument to prevent market-distorting speculation. On the contrary, by reducing trading volume they can distort pricing since individual transactions will cause greater price swings and fluctuations. But above all, not every transaction is a market-distorting speculation. Speculation is not easy to identify. For example, which is the market-distorting bet – one against or for a Greek government bankruptcy? Did the losses of the banks in the US subprime sector occur due to speculation or just bad investment decisions? What is the threshold of trading volume or frequency beyond which it is speculators and not participants with legitimate needs that drive the market price for corn, euros, or Greek government bonds?

Most importantly, however, FTTs are not the right instrument to reduce risk-taking and fragility in the financial sector, as all transactions are taxed at the same rate, independent of their risk profile. There are arguments that such a transaction tax would hit high-frequency trading hardest (Persaud 2011). But who is to say that this is the riskiest or most speculative trading? Careful analysis by Honohan and Yoder (2011) also shows that an FTT would not have impacted the CDO or CDS market in the run-up to the current crisis. The behavourial goal of taxation would thus certainly not be achieved. The revenue-raising goal, on the other hand, will certainly depend on the tax elasticities of the activities, which might be hard to estimate ex ante. Honohan and Yoder (2011) argue that even low tax rates might make certain market segments that rely on transaction-intensive trading technology unsustainable, which undermines the revenue goal.

Financial activities tax

The European Commission compares an FTT to the alternative of an FAT. This latter tax would apply to the combined profits and wage bill of financial institutions and thus be a broad tax on income generated in the financial sector. This has the advantages that the FAT does not discriminate among various financial-sector activities, and that it is able to generate considerable revenue at low tax rates. The base of the FAT amounts to the financial sector's value-added so that this tax corrects the current undertaxation of the financial sector through the VAT. On the other hand, a straight FAT does not discriminate among financial-sector activities on the basis of their contribution to financial institution risk. However, an FAT that only taxes 'excess profits', ie profits that go beyond providing equity holders with some reasonable return, could potentially help to curb financial institution risk-taking.

A recent paper by Huizinga et al (2011) explains how such a tax may affect banks' behaviour by looking at how banks change pricing behaviour across countries with different tax rates. Huizinga et al (2011) find that the burden of the international double taxation of corporate income in the banking sector is almost fully passed on to a bank's lending and depositor customers in the form of a higher bank interest margin. An estimated 86.2% of the additional international tax is reflected in higher bank interest margins abroad, while only 13.8% of this tax appears to be borne by bank shareholders.

The similarity between the FAT and the corporate income tax – they both apply to corporate profits of banks – suggests that the pass-through of an FAT to bank customers would be substantial as well. This makes the FAT a tax on bank customers rather than on bank shareholders. In effect, the FAT would appropriately lead to higher prices of services supplied by banks, reflecting the risks that banks pose to financial stability. In contrast, the incidence of an FTT is far less clear. All the same, an FTT is less likely to lead to higher prices for mainstream bank services and to curb bank risk-taking. This makes the FAT preferred to an FTT as a means to increase the contribution of the banking sector to public finances, and as a tool to reduce banking-sector risk-taking.

Evaluation

A disadvantage of the FAT is that it is does not sit well within the overall system of VAT as we know it. The FAT appropriately corrects for the undertaxation of the value-added of banks, but it does not allow for the computation of VAT input credits for businesses that are users of financial services – giving rise to a form of double taxation, as bank valued-added is taxed at the level of the bank and at the level of its business customers. For this reason, it is better to eliminate the current VAT exemption on financial services rather than to introduce a new FAT. Unfortunately, the Commission relegates possible reform of the current VAT treatment of financial services to some undefined point in the future.

As indicated, the current Commission proposal also foregoes the opportunity to bring about a common EU framework for bank levies that is sorely needed.

Thus, in its current proposal the European Commission is bypassing the first-best and second-best solutions to the current undertaxation of the EU banking sector, in the form of financial-sector VAT reform and a common framework for bank levies in the EU. Instead, the Commission is presenting us with a choice between third-best and fourth-best outcomes, ie a choice between the FAT and the FTT, and even then the Commission makes the wrong choice of favouring an FTT over a FAT. However, the Commission's current proposal to increase financial-sector taxation is unlikely to be its last one, given the already clear political opposition to an FTT in the United Kingdom among other countries. Hence, there are likely to be opportunities for the Commission to present a revised plan for financial-sector taxation in the future.

Generally, optimal policy requires a combination of financial-sector taxation and regulation. To some extent, taxation and regulation are substitutes, as both can, for instance, be used to effect higher bank capitalisation rates. However, taxation is a better tool to bring about a balance between the private benefits and social costs of bank decisions, for instance regarding their risk-taking.

This benefit of taxation over regulation, however, only materialises if there is no *quid pro quo*. Taxes or bank levies should not be interpreted as the purchases of bank liability insurance, which enables banks to take on more asset risk. A bank levy that goes into a failure resolution fund to finance future bank bailouts is the wrong step, since it turns an implicit public guarantee into an explicit one. Today the market still has to take into account a residual risk that the state does not intervene (as in the case of Lehman Brothers or some smaller banks in the US and Europe).[4] To maintain some risk for bank liability holders, new financial-sector taxes should go into the general budget rather than into earmarked resolution funds.[5]

Finally, to reduce the need for costly public bailouts in the future, it is important to improve the operation of bank recovery and resolution mechanisms in Europe. As discussed by Allen et al (2011), the current crisis has revealed important deficiencies and gaps in the European bank resolution framework. Much can be gained by moving to a common bank recovery and resolution framework that provides authorities with more options to intervene at fragile banks and to come to speedy and less costly resolutions of banks if needed.

References

Allen, Franklin, Thorsten Beck, Elena Carletti, Philip Lane, Dirk Schoenmaker, and Wolf Wagner (2011), *Cross-border banking in Europe: implications for financial stability and macroeconomic policies*, London: CEPR.

Beck, Thorsten and Thomas Losse-Müller (2011), "Financial sector taxation: balancing fairness, efficiency and stability", VoxEU.org, 31 May.

Cottarelli, Carlo (2010), "Fair and Substantial – Taxing the Financial Sector", IMFdirect.

4 For additional discussion on such a resolution fund, including a procyclical bias, see Allen et al (2011).
5 For a more detailed discussion on this, see Beck and Losse-Müller (2011).

Honohan, Patrick and Sean Yoder (2011), "Financial Transactions Tax: Panacea, Threat, or Damp Squib?", *World Bank Research Observer* 26 (1): 138-161.

Huizinga, Harry (2002), "A European VAT on Financial Services?", *Economic Policy,* October.

Huizinga, Harry, Johannes Voget, and Wolf Wagner (2011), "International taxation and cross-border banking", CEPR Working Paper 7047.

Persaud, Avinash (2011), "EU's financial transaction tax is feasible, and if set right, desirable", VoxEU.org, 30 September.

Tobin, James (1978). "A Proposal for International Monetary Reform", *Eastern Economic Journal* 4(3-4): 153–159.

About the author

Thorsten Beck is Professor of Economics and Chairman of the European Banking Center at Tilburg University, and a CEPR Research Fellow. His research and policy work has focused on international banking and corporate finance.

Harry Huizinga is Professor of International Economics in the Department of Economics at Tilburg University and a CEPR Research Fellow. His main fields of research are public economics and banking.

The future of cross-border banking

Dirk Schoenmaker
Duisenberg School of Finance and VU University Amsterdam

Responses to the financial crisis have largely been along national lines. Governments rescued banks headquartered within their borders, and supervisors are requiring banks to match their assets and liabilities at a national level. This chapter says stable cross-border banking is incompatible with national financial supervision, which means the European banking market needs European authorities.

International trade and the of multinational business operations have traditionally been facilitated by international banks. The client-pull hypothesis (Grosse and Goldberg 1991) argues that a bank's international clientele provide an incentive for internationalisation by that bank, since the financial system of the foreign country might the sophistication desired by the bank's clientele.

Following the financial crises, the international business model of banks is under pressure. Governments' bank rescue operations were performed on a national basis in the first financial crisis of 2007-09. US TARP funds were, for example, only available for US-headquartered banks. European banks with significant operations in the US were not eligible. By the same token, European banks were supported by their respective home governments. In the case of truly cross-border banks, such as Fortis, the banks were split and resolved on national lines.

The supervisory response to this national fiscal backstop has been to reinforce supervisors' national mandates, while paying lipservice to international cooperation with non-binding Memoranda of Understanding (MoUs). In the second financial crisis starting in 2010, banks are required by their supervisors to match their assets and liabilities on national lines. So a French bank with liabilities in the US is required to keep matching assets in US, while having a US dollar shortage at home. The same tends to happen within Europe. When a Dutch bank is collecting deposits via the Internet in Spain, the local supervisor starts asking for matching assets in Spain. Local holdings of liquidity and capital are suboptimal (Allen et al 2011). The Internal Market in Banking is being reversed.

What does theory say?

The financial trilemma indicates that the three objectives of financial stability, cross-border banking, and national financial supervision are not compatible (Schoenmaker 2011). One has to give. The trilemma makes clear that policymakers have to make a choice on cross-border banking. While we were slowly evolving towards European financial supervision with the establishment of the new European Supervisory Authorities and the European Systemic Risk Board, the financial crisis has thrown us back towards national supervision.

What are the facts?

De Haan et al (forthcoming) examine the developments of large banks in the aftermath of the first financial crisis. They select the 60 largest banks on the basis of Tier 1 capital, as reported in the Top 1,000 world banks rankings by *The Banker.* The dataset is divided into three samples of top European banks, top American banks, and top Asian banks.

Table 1 reports the geographical segmentation of these banks for the years 2006 to 2009. European banks are the most international, with close to 50% of business abroad. This may be due to the integrated European banking market. But even when looking at their business outside the region, European banks are the most international – 25% of their business is in the rest of the world. American banks are catching up; their business in the rest of the world rose from 14% in 2006 to 21% in 2009. So, the European and

American banks have maintained their international outlook throughout the 2007-09 financial crisis.

The picture is very different for the Asian-Pacific banks. They used to have a very domestic orientation, which was reinforced over the last several years. Business in the rest of the world declined from 13% in 2006 to 8% in 2009. Although the Asian-Pacific banks are least affected by the US-originated financial crisis, they seem to be retrenching from the international scene. The composition of the top Asian-Pacific banks is shifting from the major Japanese banks to the major Chinese banks, which have an even stronger domestic orientation than Japanese ones.

Table 1. Development of international banking by continent, 2006-09

Continent	2006			2007			2008			2009		
	h	r	w	h	r	w	h	r	w	h	r	w
Europe	25	23	25	52	22	25	51	21	28	52	22	26
Americas	78	8	14	75	10	15	73	9	18	72	7	21
Asia-Pacific	82	5	13	83	6	11	82	7	11	85	7	8

Notes: Share of business in home country (h), rest of region (r) and rest of world (w) of the top banks by continent. The shares add up to 100%.

Source: De Haan et al (forthcoming).

While European and American banks have maintained their international business after the first financial crisis, more recent anecdotal evidence of the ongoing second financial crisis indicates that supervisors are forcing banks to maintain local holdings of liquidity and capital. What are the costs of maintaining separate capital and liquidity buffers at national standalone subsidiaries? In a first study on this topic, Cerutti et al (2010) simulate the potential capital needs of 25 major European cross-border banking groups resulting from a credit shock affecting their affiliates in central, eastern, and southern Europe. The simulations show that under ring-fencing (standalone subsidiaries) sample banks' aggregate capital needs are 1.5 to three times higher than in the case of no ring-fencing.

The way forward

If policymakers seek to enhance global banking, then the international community must provide a higher and better-coordinated level of fiscal support than it has in the past (Obstfeld 2011). Capital or loans to troubled financial institutions (as well as sovereign countries) imply a credit risk that ultimately must be lodged somewhere. Expanded international lending facilities, including an expanded IMF, cannot remain unconditionally solvent absent an expanded level of fiscal backup.

The same point obviously applies to the European framework. If policymakers want to preserve the Internal Market in Banking, then the institutional framework must be improved along the following lines:

- **Supervision**: The European Banking Authority must get the cross-border banks under its supervisory wings. Supervision would then move from a national mandate (with loose coordination) to a European mandate.
- **Lender of last resort**: The European Central Bank is operating as the de facto lender of last resort for the European banking system.
- **Deposit insurance**: Deposit insurance for cross-border banks should be based on a European footing.
- **Resolution**: A European resolution authority should be established to resolve troubled cross-border banks. Ex ante burden-sharing rules are needed to raise the required funds for resolving cross-border banks (Goodhart and Schoenmaker 2009).

As suggested by Allen et al (2011), the latter two functions can be combined within some kind of European equivalent of the FDIC. The EU would then get a European deposit insurance fund with resolution powers. The fund would be fed through regular risk-based deposit insurance premiums with a fiscal backstop of national governments based on a precommitted burden sharing key.

References

Allen, F, T Beck, E Carletti, P Lane, D Schoenmaker and W Wagner (2011), *Cross-Border Banking in Europe: Implications for Financial Stability and Macroeconomic Policies*, CEPR eReport. London: Centre for Economic Policy Research.

Cerutti, E, A Ilyina, Y Makarova, and C Schmieder (2010), "Bankers Without Borders? Implications of Ring-Fencing for European Cross-Border Banks," IMF Working Paper 10/247.

De Haan, J, S Oosterloo, and D Schoenmaker (forthcoming), *Financial Markets and Institutions: A European Text*, 2nd Edition, Cambridge: Cambridge University Press.

Goodhart, C and D Schoenmaker (2009), "Fiscal Burden Sharing in Cross-Border Banking Crises", *International Journal of Central Banking* 5, 141-165.

Grosse, R and LG Goldberg (1991), "Foreign bank activity in the United States: An analysis by country of origin", *Journal of Banking & Finance* 15, 1092–1112.

Obstfeld, M (2011), "International Liquidity: The Fiscal Dimension", NBER Working Paper No. 17379.

Schoenmaker, D (2011), "The Financial Trilemma", *Economics Letters* 111, 57-59.

About the author

Dirk Schoenmaker is Dean of the Duisenberg School of Finance and Professor of Finance, Banking and Insurance at the VU University Amsterdam. He has published in the areas of central banking, financial supervision and stability, and European financial integration.

The changing role of emerging-market banks

Neeltje van Horen
De Nederlandsche Bank

The global financial crisis has hurt banks in both advanced and emerging economies, but this chapter says the turmoil has favored the emerging-market entities in relative terms. It predicts a growing role for emerging-market banks in the global financial system, particularly in their own regions.

The global financial crisis has had a major impact on banks worldwide. While some banks are faced with major restructurings (either voluntary or imposed by governments), (almost) all banks will have to make adjustments in order to comply with Basel III and other, country-specific regulatory measures. The changes induced by the crisis, however, will have a very different impact on advanced country banks compared to emerging-market banks. How will this shift in balance impact the global financial system?

Crouching tiger, hidden dragon

Although many in the West are not familiar with emerging-market banks, they are by no means small. In fact, the world's biggest bank in market value is China's ICBC. The global top 25 includes eight emerging-market banks. Among these, three other Chinese banks (China Construction Bank, Agricultural Bank of China, and Bank of China), three Brazilian banks (Itaú Unibanco, Banco do Brasil, and Banco Bradesco) and one Russian bank (Sberbank). While excess optimism might have inflated these market values, these banks are large with respect to other measures as well. In terms of assets all these banks are in the top 75 worldwide, with all four Chinese banks in the top 20.

Furthermore, in 2010 emerging-market banks as a group accounted for roughly 30% of global profits, a third of global revenues and half of tier 1 capital.

Not only are emerging-market banks already substantially large; they are catching up rapidly. Asset growth has been impressive in many emerging markets. Although China again tops the ranks, other emerging markets have seen impressive increases in bank assets as well. While emerging-market banks already grew faster than their advanced-country counterparts prior to 2007, the financial crisis has accelerated this trend. The expected continued growth of emerging-market banks, and the likely stagnation (or even contraction) of advanced-country banks, many of which still face multiple risks, implies that the relative importance of emerging-market banks will quickly grow.

Differences that count

Several factors make it easier for emerging-market banks to weather the storm caused by the financial crisis. First, loan-to-deposit ratios in general are very low due to the net saving position of these countries. This sheltered emerging-market banking systems to a large extent from the collapse of the interbank market and reduced the need for substantial deleveraging. This allows them now to continue lending using a stable and often growing source of deposit funding. Second, most emerging-market banks already have high capital ratios, limiting pressures for balance sheet adjustments. In addition, the new capital rules under Basel III are likely to be much less painful for these banks as they typically have less risky assets and their investment-banking business tends to be small.

Equally important, emerging-market banks face a very different situation in their domestic market compared to their advanced-country peers. First, a large part of the population in the emerging world is still unbanked. This provides for ample growth opportunities in these markets. In contrast, due to overall economic weakness and ongoing deleveraging among firms and households expected credit growth in advanced economies is low. Second, the macroeconomic outlook in these countries is much better than that of advanced countries. Not faced with major sovereign debt problems, nor large current-account deficits, most emerging markets are on pretty solid footing. Even though they will not be isolated from the problems in Europe and the United States, the dependency of these markets on the West has diminished in recent years.

International expansion

Due to sheer size, emerging-market banks almost undoubtedly will soon become important players in the world's financial system. It is less clear, however, how far their global reach is going to extend. With still a large part of the population unbanked, most emerging-market banks face pressures at home to increase lending which reduces funds available for foreign expansion. Furthermore, an important share of excess deposits is stuck in sleepy state banks that have shown very limited interest in expanding abroad. In addition, many emerging-market banks have only limited provisions set aside, especially compared to advanced country banks, and therefore are facing pressures to increase their bad debt reserves. Finally, regulators might oppose foreign adventures as the use of domestic deposits to finance a subsidiary overseas exposes the bank to foreign-exchange and counterparty risk.

At the same time a number of factors could as well push these banks into increasing their global presence. First, even with the caveats described above, the funding position of most large emerging-market banks looks good, providing them with relatively large amounts of funds compared to their advanced country counterparts. Furthermore, a number of these banks are highly profitable which allows them to invest and at the same times gives them a buffer to absorb potential losses. Both factors provide emerging-market banks with the means to seize opportunities when advanced-country banks, in need to consolidate, are either forced or voluntarily sell some of their subsidiaries. Further, an increasing number of emerging-market companies are establishing a presence overseas, providing emerging-market banks with opportunities to extend their foreign network in order to service their domestic customers abroad.[1] Finally, a substantial number of emerging-market banks are no strangers to setting up branches or subsidiaries in other countries. In fact, in 2009 close to 30% of the foreign banks were owned by emerging-market banks.[2] This shows that these banks do have the knowledge and expertise to undertake and manage overseas operations.

Staying close to home

Taking stock, it is to be expected that in the coming years emerging-market banks not only will grow in their domestic market but also will expand their global reach. However, this expansion is likely to be confined to the geographical region of the bank's headquarters. Research has shown that closeness to their clients makes it easier for banks to do business.[3] So profit margins are likely relatively high for emerging-market banks in other emerging markets. Indeed, if we look at the previous expansion of emerging-market banks, 70% of their investments tend to be in countries within their own geographical region.[4] Furthermore, with a fully developed banking system, sovereign debt problems, and low expected economic growth, profits are unlikely to be reaped in advanced countries, providing another reason why investments in other emerging markets are more likely. In addition, the regulatory crackdown in advanced countries, caused by some cross-border bank failures, might make it hard for emerging-market banks to set up a branch or subsidiary in these countries.

With advanced-country banks trying to adjust to the new rules of the game, it is unlikely that many of these banks will remain active investors in the near future. Banks from emerging markets, being in a much better financial position, are likely to step

1 It has long been established that banks tend to follow their customers abroad (see, among others, Grosse and Goldberg 1991 and Brealey and Kaplanis 1996.)

2 Source: Foreign banking database (Claessens and van Horen 2011).

3 A number of studies show that banks tend to invest in countries that are geographically, legally and/or institutionally close (Galindo et al 2003, Focarelli and Pozzolo 2005). In addition, De Haas and Van Horen (2011) provide evidence that closeness is an important determinant of cross-border lending stability in times of crises.

4 Source: Foreign banking database (Claessens and van Horen 2011).

into the void left by advanced country banks, increasing their relative importance as foreign investors. The global financial system is therefore likely to witness a shift towards a stronger dominance by emerging-market banks, especially within their own geographical regions.

Disclaimer: The views expressed in this column are those of the author only and do not necessarily reflect the views of the De Nederlandsche Bank, the European System of Central Banks, or their Boards.

References

Brealey, Richard and EC Kaplanis (1996) "The Determination of Foreign Banking Location," *Journal of International Money and Finance* 15: 577–597.

Claessens, Stijn and Neeltje van Horen (2011) "Trends in Foreign Banking: A Database on Bilateral Foreign Bank Ownership", mimeo, International Monetary Fund and De Nederlandsche Bank.

De Haas, Ralph and Neeltje van Horen (2011) "Running for the Exit: International Banks and Crisis Transmission", DNB Working Paper No. 279.

Focarelli, Dario and Alberto F Pozzolo (2005) "Where do Banks Expand Abroad? An Empirical Analysis", *Journal of Business* 78: 2435–2463.

Galindo, Arturo, Alejandro Micco, and César Serra (2003) "Better the Devil That You Know: Evidence on Entry Costs Faced by Foreign Banks", Inter-American Development Bank Working Paper No. 477.

Grosse, Robert and Lawrence Goldberg (1991) "Foreign Bank Activity in the United States: An Analysis by Country of Origin", *Journal of Banking and Finance* 15: 1092–1112.

About the author

Neeltje van Horen is a Senior Economist at the Research Department of the Dutch Central Bank and a Researcher at the Economics Department of the University of Amsterdam. Her research focuses mainly on international finance and international financial markets and institutions. She has published articles on foreign banking, financial crises, contagion and financial integration.

Finance, long-run growth, and economic opportunity

Ross Levine
Brown University

Financial systems support and spur economic growth. But does financial innovation foster financial development? While recent innovations have done damage, this chapter says the long-run story is that financial innovation is essential for economic growth.

Finance is powerful. The financial system can be an engine of economic prosperity – or a destructive cause of economic decline and misery. The impact of the financial system on the rest of the economy depends on how it mobilises savings, allocates those savings, monitors the use of those funds by firms and individuals, pools and diversifies risk, including liquidity risk, and eases the exchange of goods and services.

When financial systems perform well, they tend to promote growth and expand economic opportunities. For example, when banks screen borrowers effectively and identify firms with the most promising prospects, this is a first step in boosting productivity growth. When financial markets and institutions mobilise savings from disparate households to invest in these promising projects, this represents a second crucial step in fostering growth. When financial institutions monitor the use of investments and scrutinise their managerial performance, this is another essential ingredient in boosting the operational efficiency of corporations, reducing waste and fraud, and spurring economic growth. When securities markets ease the diversification of risk, this encourages investment in higher-return projects that might be shunned without effective risk management vehicles. And when financial systems lower transaction costs, this facilitates trade and specialisation, which are fundamental inputs into technological innovation and economic growth.

But when financial systems perform poorly, they tend to hinder economic growth and curtail economic opportunities. For example, if financial systems simply collect funds with one hand and pass them along to cronies, the wealthy, and the politically connected with the other hand, this produces a less efficient allocation of resources, implying slower economic growth. If financial institutions fail to exert sound corporate governance, this makes it easier for managers to pursue projects that benefit themselves rather than the firm and the overall economy. Similarly, well-functioning financial systems allocate capital based on a person's ideas and abilities, not on family wealth and political connections. But, poorly functioning financial systems become an effective tool for restricting credit – and hence opportunity – to the already rich and powerful.

As stressed by King and Levine (1993), Levine (2005), and Levine and Zervos (1998), the financial system exerts this powerful influence over the economy primarily by affecting the quality of capital allocation, not the quantity of investment. Thus, finance should not be viewed as a plumbing system, where pouring more credit in one end yields more growth at the other. Rather, finance functions as an economy's central nervous system, choosing where to allocate resources. It is the incentives shaping these choices that influence economic growth.

Evidence

A growing and diverse body of empirical research produces a remarkably consistent, though by no means unanimous, narrative. The services provided by banks exert a first-order impact on (1) the rate of long-run economic growth, primarily by affecting the allocation of capital, and (2) the distribution of income, primarily by affecting the earnings of lower-income individuals. This message emerges from cross-country analyses, panel techniques that exploit both cross-country differences and changes in national performance over time, microeconomic studies that examine the underlying mechanisms through which finance may influence economic growth, and individual country cases.

For example, measures of the level of bank development in 1960 predict the growth rate of real per capita GDP over the next forty years even after controlling for cross-country differences in initial income and education, national differences in measures of the openness to international trade, inflation, fiscal deficits, and after conditioning on indicators of political stability, as shown by King and Levine (1993). Furthermore, the close association between bank development and long-run growth runs primarily through the allocation of credit, not through the overall rate of investment.

Research also shows that bank development disproportionately helps the poor (Beck et al 2011). Improvements in the functioning of banks reduce income inequality. Moreover, this tightening in the distribution of income does not happen by making the rich poorer, but rather primarily by boosting the incomes of the poor.

Securities markets matter too. As shown by Levine and Zervos (1998), better-functioning equity markets improve the efficiency of capital allocation, boosting growth. Thus, securities markets are not simply casinos where the rich come to place their bets. They too can affect both the allocation of capital and the availability of economic opportunities.

Financial innovation

How does financial innovation fit into the process of economic growth? Given the roles of credit default swaps, collateralized debt obligations, and other new financial instruments in the recent financial crisis, financial innovation has developed a bad reputation. From this perspective financial innovations are mechanisms for fooling investors, circumventing regulatory intent, and boosting the bonuses of financiers without enhancing the quality of the services provided by the financial services industry. This is part of the story. Financial innovation can be a powerful source of economic instability, stagnation, and misery. But this is only an incomplete part of the story.

A longer-run consideration of financial development suggests that financial innovation is essential for growth. Adam Smith argued that economic growth is a process in which production become increasingly specialized and technologies more complex. As firms become more complex, however, the old financial system becomes less effective at screening and monitoring firms. Therefore, without corresponding innovations in finance that match the increases in complexity associated with economic growth, the quality of financial services diminishes, slowing future growth.

Several examples from history illustrate the crucial role of financial innovation in sustaining economic growth as noted by Laeven et al (2011). Consider first the financial impediments to railroad expansion in the 19th century. The novelty and complexity of railroads made pre-existing financial systems ineffective at screening and monitoring them. Although prominent local investors with close ties to those operating the railroad were the primary sources of capital for railroads during the early decades of this new technology, this reliance on local finance restricted growth.

So financiers innovated. Specialized financiers and investment banks emerged to mobilise capital from individuals, to screen and invest in railroads, and to monitor the use of those investments, often by serving on the boards of directors of railroad corporations. Based on their expertise and reputation, these investment banks mobilized funds from wealthy investors, evaluated proposals from railroads, allocated capital, and governed the operations of railroad companies for investors. And since the geographical size and complexity of railroads made it difficult for investors to collect, organise, and assess price, usage, breakdown, and repair information, financiers developed new accounting and financial reporting methods.

Next, consider the information technology revolution of the 20th century, which could not have been financed with the financial system that fuelled the railroad revolution of the 19th century. Indeed, as nascent high-tech information and communication firms struggled to emerge in the 1970s and 1980s, traditional commercial banks were reluctant to finance them because these new firms did not yet generate sufficient cash flows to cover loan payments and the firms were run by scientists with little experience in operating profitable companies. Conventional debt and equity markets were also wary because the technologies were too complex for investors to evaluate.

Again, financiers innovated. Venture capital firms arose to screen entrepreneurs and provide technical, managerial, and financial advice to new high-technology firms. In many cases, venture capitalists had become wealthy through their own successful high-tech innovations, which provided a basis of expertise for evaluating and guiding new entrepreneurs. In terms of funding, venture capitalists typically took large, private equity stakes that established a long-term commitment to the enterprise, and they generally became active investors, taking seats on the board of directors and helping to solve managerial and financial problems.

Finally, consider the biotechnology revolution of the 21st century, for which the venture capital modality did not work well. Venture capitalists could not effectively screen biotech firms because of the scientific breadth of biotechnologies, which frequently require inputs from biologists, chemists, geneticists, engineers, bioroboticists, as well as experts on the myriad of laws, regulations, and commercial barriers associated with successfully bringing new medical products to market. It was unfeasible to house all of this expertise in banks or venture capital firms. Again, a new technology promised growth, but the existing financial system could not fuel it.

Yet again, financiers innovated. They formed new financial partnerships with the one kind of organisation with the breadth of skills to screen biotech firms – large pharmaceutical companies. Pharmaceutical companies employ, or are in regular contact with, a large assortment of scientists and engineers, have close connections with those delivering medical products to customers, and employ lawyers well-versed in drug regulations. Furthermore, when an expert pharmaceutical company invests in a biotech firm this encourages others to invest in the firm as well. Without financial innovation, improvements in diagnostic and surgical procedures, prosthetic devices, parasite-resistant crops, and other innovations linked to biotechnology would almost certainly be occurring at a far slower pace.

Conclusion

The operation of the financial system exerts a powerful influence on economic growth and the opportunities available to individuals. Well-functioning financial systems allocate resources to those with the best ideas and entrepreneurial skills, enhancing efficiency and expanding economic horizons. Poorly functioning financial systems funnel credit to those with strong political and social connections, with harmful ramifications on economic welfare.

Author's Note: This paper draws liberally from "Regulating Finance and Regulators to Promote Growth," which was presented at the Federal Reserve Bank of Kansas City's Symposium, Achieving Maximum Long-Run Growth, which was held in Jackson Hole, Wyoming on August 25-27, 2011 and will be published in the proceedings of that symposium.

References

Beck, Thorsten, Ross Levine, and Alexey Levkov (2010) "Big Bad Banks? The Winners and Losers from US Branch Deregulation." *Journal of Finance* 65: 1637-1667.

King, Robert G, and Ross Levine (1993) "Finance and Growth: Schumpeter Might Be Right." *Quarterly Journal of Economics* 108: 717-38.

Laeven, Luc, Ross Levine, and Stelios Michalopoulos (2011) "Financial and Innovation and Endogenous Growth." Brown University, mimeo.

Levine, Ross (2005) "Finance and Growth: Theory and Evidence." in *Handbook of Economic Growth*, Eds., Aghion, P. and S. Durlauf, 1A, pp. 865-934, North-Holland Elsevier, Amsterdam.

Levine, Ross, and Sara Zervos (1998) "Stock Markets, Banks, and Economic Growth." *American Economic Review* 88: 537-558.

About the author

Ross Levine is the Harrison S. Kravis University Professor at Brown University. A frequent consultant at the International Monetary Fund and the World Bank, he is an Associate Editor of the *Journal of Economic Growth* and the *Journal of Financial Intermediation.* After working at the Board of Governors of the Federal Reserve System for three years, Dr. Levine moved to the World Bank in 1990. There he participated and managed a number of research and operational programs. He received his Ph.D. in economics from UCLA in 1987.